AMERICA'S HIDDEN
ECONOMIC ENGINES

WORK AND **LEARNING SERIES**

Series edited by Robert B. Schwartz and Nancy Hoffman

OTHER BOOKS IN THIS SERIES

Schooling in the Workplace
Nancy Hoffman

Youth, Education, and the Role of Society
Robert Halpern

Learning for Careers
Nancy Hoffman and Robert B. Schwartz

Vocational Education and Training for a Global Economy
Edited by Marc S. Tucker

Career Pathways in Action
Edited by Robert B. Schwartz and Amy Loyd

Career Pathways for All Youth
Stephen F. Hamilton

Teaching Students About the World of Work
Edited by Nancy Hoffman and Michael Lawrence Collins

AMERICA'S HIDDEN ECONOMIC ENGINES

*How Community Colleges
Can Drive Shared Prosperity*

Robert B. Schwartz
Rachel Lipson

Editors

HARVARD EDUCATION PRESS
CAMBRIDGE MA

Third Printing, 2023

Paperback ISBN 978-1-68253-816-6

Library of Congress Cataloging-in-Publication Data is on file.

Published by Harvard Education Press,
an imprint of the Harvard Education Publishing Group
Harvard Education Press
8 Story Street
Cambridge, MA 02138

Cover Design: Wilcox Design
Cover Images: -VICTOR-/DigitalVision Vectors via Getty Images;
            ilyast/DigitalVision Vectors via Getty Images

The typefaces in this book are Adobe Garamond Pro and Helvetica Neue.

CONTENTS

SERIES PREFACE

Nancy Hoffman

That community colleges are the "hidden engines" that can drive shared prosperity would be a surprise to many. *College*, to the general public, means a four-year institution, and yet the 1,100 community colleges across the nation enroll 40 percent of all undergraduates and 50 percent of Black, Hispanic, and Native American college students. They serve working learners: 62 percent of full-time and 72 percent of part-time students have jobs, many balancing school, family, and full-time work. Students come to community college not because it's what you do after high school but seeking a better life, a better income, greater economic security, and the greater self-confidence that comes with having a degree. Within the higher education ecosystem, as I frequently say, community colleges are there "to teach everything to anybody."

As curators of the Work and Learning series, Bob Schwartz and I are proud to have contributed to the emerging story of these critical institutions. *America's Hidden Economic Engines: How Community Colleges Can Drive Shared Prosperity* profiles five community colleges that stand out from the already impressive crowd of institutions. These case studies document how these hidden gems lead the way where other colleges are trying to go: they collaborate closely with their regional businesses to provide the education and training needed to fill current labor market needs while also preparing a next-generation talent pipeline for the future. Located in contrasting geographies from Virginia to Mississippi to Arizona, they have tailored their programs to meet the unique needs of regional business and industry while also providing access to broader opportunities to pursue the full associate's or bachelor's degree. These colleges treat employers as true partners, codevelopers, and co-owners of programs along with faculty and staff. As such, they might be called *dual-client successes*—meeting student needs for higher income and career advancement and simultaneously strengthening regional economies.

In the US, community colleges serve as the critical link between education and business and are the closest institutions we have to the strongest non-US vocational institutions that inspired Bob's and my contributions to the career pathways movement. After Bob and I finished two stints working as consultants for the Organization for Economic Co-operation and Development (OECD) on its multicountry study of vocational education,[1] we came back to the US with deep admiration for the ways in which other countries prepare sixteen- to twenty-year-olds for the labor force. In Switzerland, for example, 70 percent of sixteen- to twenty-year-olds spend three or four years in a well-structured apprenticeship combining learning at a workplace with aligned academics and culminating in an industry credential that is portable throughout Europe. Our OECD experience helped inspire the creation of the Pathways to Prosperity Network (Pathways Network), profiled in our 2017 book *Learning for Careers*. The Pathways Network, now working in sixty regions across the US with leadership from Jobs for the Future, creates pathway systems that span grades 11 through 14 and are designed to provide all students with a first postsecondary credential with value in the labor market.

Two books in the Work and Learning series tell what's to be learned from strong vocational education and training systems in other countries: In 2011, Harvard Education Press published my book, *Schooling in the Workplace: How Six of the World's Best Vocational Education Systems Prepare Young People for Jobs and Life*, the first book in the series. In 2019, Harvard Education Press then published Mark S. Tucker's *Vocational Education and Training for a Global Economy: Lessons from Four Countries*. Two takeaways from these books stood out as inspirations: first, at sixteen, young people are developmentally ready to try out adult work roles and flourish when challenged and supported in the workplace; and second, in well-functioning economies, education and training programs are closely aligned with labor market needs—both immediate and future. The profiled community colleges in *America's Hidden Economic Engines* reproduce some of the key qualities of non-US vocational institutions.

One additional book in the series, *Teaching Students About the World of Work: A Challenge to Postsecondary Educators* (2019), argues that community colleges must do much more to ensure that students address questions that range from why people work to how labor markets operate to race, gender, and power dynamics in the workplace. Paired with *America's Hidden Economic Engines*, this book provides an overview of topics that community colleges would do well to emphasize in the curriculum as they take steps to move toward greater and more powerful partnerships with their business communities.

A further note on the series: each of the six US-focused books in the series uses lessons from outside the US to ask how our institutions can foster successful career development and lead to economically secure and thriving regional economies and communities. Each book comes at this question from a different perspective.

Two of the three student-focused books, Robert Halpern's *Youth, Education, and the Role of Society* (2013) and *Striving to Thriving in Life and Work: Youth Occupational Identity* (working title, forthcoming 2023) attend to youth development, discussing, respectively, how little heed high schools pay to activities that would help students prepare for adulthood; and how young adults age sixteen to twenty-one, particularly Black and Latinx youth, speak about themselves and the adult lives they want to live. Another book that also pairs nicely with *America's Hidden Economic Engines*: *Career Pathways in Action* (2019) is a series of case studies of successful grade 9 through 14 career pathways policies and programs in six states and regions, highlighting the role of community colleges in each case. Finally, Stephen F. Hamilton's *Career Pathways for All Youth* (2020), which profiles on-the-ground implementation of the School-to-Work Opportunities Act of 1994, and *Learning for Careers* (2017), about the career pathways "remake" of the 2010s, tell contrasting stories and provide historical context for today's career pathways movement. Circling back to community colleges, one major difference between the school-to-work models of the 1990s and the career pathways movement today is that the former did not call out the role of community colleges, while the latter features, as a "best bet" requirement for a good job, a first postsecondary degree or certification awarded by a community college.

FOREWORD

Harry J. Holzer

For years now, a number of serious problems have plagued both workers and employers in the US job market.

For one thing, worker earnings have been mostly stagnant for several decades, and inequality in earnings is very high. While those with bachelor's degrees or higher have enjoyed earnings gains over time, only about one-third of all Americans have such degrees.

Others attend community colleges, and on average the associate's degrees and certificates they can earn can be quite valuable. But community colleges struggle with a number of problems: completion rates are very low (just 40 percent after six years); the market value of associate's degrees in liberal arts, which 40 percent or more of graduates attain in some states, is also low; and many lower-income students default on the loans they take out to help pay for their studies, especially noncompleters. These problems are most serious for low-income students or those of color.

And many employers are frustrated as well. They face worker shortages in many occupations, even those requiring skills short of bachelor's degrees. In a range of industries, like healthcare, construction, advanced manufacturing, information technology, and transportation and logistics, employers have difficulty hiring and retaining workers in jobs where specific skills are needed.

The requisite skills often exceed what can be provided purely through on-the-job training—and even where it can be provided, many employers either lack the knowledge of how to provide such training efficiently or fear that their training investments will be wasted if and when their employees leave to work somewhere else. The US lacks the strong systems of apprenticeship found in many European countries. And as baby boomers continue to retire, these skill shortages in the US will likely grow more serious.

At the same time, we find evidence of successful job training for both workers and employers in a number of recent studies. *Sector-based training*, in which employers partner with training providers and nonprofit intermediaries to create programs that meet their skills needs, has generated high completion rates and strong earnings gains for workers in a number of well-known programs, such as Per Scholas, Year Up, and the Wisconsin Regional Training Partnership.

But these programs are often considered "little gems" that reach far too few students and employers. Even when they are replicated, as most are now trying to do, the numbers of trained workers they will generate are far too small to begin solving the problems of labor market inequality and skilled worker shortages. Indeed, only community colleges have the infrastructure, funding, and scale to reach the millions of workers and many thousands of employers in high-demand industries who need such training now. The challenge, however, is that community colleges are multipurpose institutions—and while nearly all community college presidents would list workforce development as one of their purposes, a much smaller number would identify workforce development as core to the institution's mission.

In late 2021, Harvard University's Project on Workforce set out to identify and profile five community colleges that met two criteria: they prioritize career advancement for all learners across all programs, credit and noncredit alike; and through their close partnerships with regional employers and programmatic alignment with regional labor market needs, they have positioned themselves to be key players in their region's workforce and economic development ecosystem.

The five selected colleges—Lorain County Community College (LCCC) in Ohio; Mississippi Gulf Coast Community College (MGCCC) in Mississippi; Northern Virginia Community College (NOVA) in the Washington, DC, suburbs; Pima Community College (Pima) in Arizona; and San Jacinto Community College (San Jac) in Texas—are located in different regions and serve quite different industries and demographic groups of students. Yet each has managed to align its programs closely enough with regional labor market needs to provide key industries with a steady flow of well-prepared workers, thereby serving both the career advancement goals of its students and the needs of the regional economy.

In this timely and important volume coedited by Harvard's Rachel Lipson and Bob Schwartz, the case studies of the five colleges and the excellent cross-case analytic chapter by Lipson give readers a strong feel for what seems to work in each institution and each locale. Success was not achieved quickly at any college; each required a process of trial and error, often over a period of many years, to address the many challenges of providing effective workforce training to their local populations. And what emerges across the five colleges is not a cookie-cutter model of what works, but rather a set of carefully developed responses to ongoing challenges that are somewhat shared across the five institutions, but also specific to the particular characteristics of their regions.

The differences in population demographics and industry needs for workers are easy to document. For instance, NOVA is a majority minority-serving institution located in a relatively high-income county where the demand for workers with IT skills is growing exponentially. LCCC is in Metro Cleveland, which is transitioning from older to more advanced manufacturing. MGCCC has a large African American population and must serve somewhat unique industries like shipbuilding. San Jac in Greater Houston serves a substantial Hispanic population and works closely with major regional employers in fields like maritime and petrochemicals. Finally, Pima is in the Tucson area, with a heavily Hispanic population and industries like aerospace advanced manufacturing to serve.

Despite being located in a set of regions with highly diverse demographic and industrial profiles, the community colleges must also wrestle with a common set of challenges that are well-known to workforce development specialists and analysts. These challenges include the following:

- How should the college promote both student *enrollment* and program *completion*? Enrollment sometimes lags behind in programs for industries like advanced manufacturing, where students (and especially women) still perceive jobs as blue-collar work for males in overalls, rather than the much more technical and well-compensated jobs that now require very different kinds of training. But these programs also struggle with low completion among enrolled students, who often enter with weak academic preparation and/or vague plans for their careers that interfere with academic and career success.

- How can these programs consistently engage local employers in key industries, whose input they need to craft curricula that remain relevant to employer skill needs, but whose assistance they also need to generate instructors for key classes, work-based learning opportunities, and jobs for their graduates?

- How can the colleges maintain both for-credit and not-for-credit programs, each of which serves different student and industry needs? Students in for-credit programs can more easily obtain two-year or four-year degrees, rather than certificates alone. But the not-for-credit programs are sometimes more nimble and less bureaucratic in their responses to changing industry skill needs (when, for example, some older jobs become automated) and also better suit students who are working full-time.

- How can both for-credit and not-for-credit programs be financed at the institution and for students, given that only the for-credit students qualify for federal funding (like Pell Grants and federal loans) under Title IV of the Higher Education Act?

The case study chapters illustrate some common themes and approaches across the five colleges for addressing these shared concerns. For instance, each college provides career planning services to improve enrollments and help students focus more quickly on career goals; each engages with key local employers to gain information that is relevant for curriculum development and to secure commitments to hire students; and each tries to incorporate both for-credit and not-for-credit programs into their career pathways. Each realizes the importance of key support services, like childcare and tutoring, to improve retention and completion rates.

At the same time, we also find many innovative ideas and approaches that individual colleges have developed—sometimes painstakingly over time—to address these shared challenges or their particular needs. For instance, NOVA makes heavy use of labor market data in fashioning the programs and curricula that will serve the rapidly changing IT sector in the DC region; MGCCC relies on data analytics to illuminate which students are having difficulty passing gateway classes or otherwise progressing on their routes to credential completion; Pima and LCCC have developed multiple, flexible pathways that integrate for-credit and not-for-credit classes and programs while helping to blur the lines between them; and San Jac has produced economic development partnerships with key local industries and incubators for noncredit students to explore more career opportunities in these fields. Several institutions have also explored innovative ways of funding the not-for-credit programs, such as regional collaboratives with local industry support. In many such cases, it is also not just *what* colleges do, but very much *how* they do it, that can determine success or failure.

The chapters of this book thus illustrate how a common set of challenges for workforce development appear even across very diverse settings; and their responses to these challenges contain both common approaches (like employer engagement and use of data) and innovations that each site has undertaken. The book should thus prove very helpful to community college administrators who must wrestle with these same challenges each day, as well as to state workforce and economic development leaders who are trying to ensure better economic opportunities for local residents and the talent needed by local industries to remain engaged in their region. Lipson and Schwartz and their graduate student case writers have done the fields of workforce development and higher education an enormous service by producing this volume of very relevant case studies. By highlighting a range of innovative practices to common challenges in diverse demographic and industrial settings, the studies here should help inform both research and practice by workforce development analysts for years to come.

Harry J. Holzer is the John LaFarge Jr. SJ Professor of Public Policy at Georgetown University's McCourt School of Public Policy, a Nonresident Senior Fellow at Brookings, and an Institute Fellow at the American Institute for Research in Washington, DC. He is a former Chief Economist for the US Department of Labor.

Introduction

Robert B. Schwartz

This book is a product of Harvard University's Project on Workforce (HPoW), a collaboration among faculty at Harvard Business School, Harvard Graduate School of Education, and Harvard Kennedy School. The two of us serve respectively as director (Lipson) and senior advisor (Schwartz) at HPoW. Our faculty team came together in 2019 with a shared goal of building a research and policy agenda to help shape a postsecondary system of the future that creates more and better pathways to economic mobility and forges smoother transitions between education and careers.

One core belief that binds our HPoW team together is that America's 1,000+ community and technical colleges must play a central role in any national strategy to strengthen and expand pathways to economic mobility for both young people and adults. These colleges serve both young people and adults most in need of career preparation; they are low-cost and open access; they are within commuting distance for all but the most rural communities; and they represent by far the largest public investment in infrastructure devoted to providing skills and credentials for those who most need them to get on a path to economic self-sufficiency. At their best, community colleges are the most nimble, flexible, market-oriented institutions in our higher education system, working closely with employers to meet regional labor market demands.

The reason we use the qualifier "at their best" in describing the role community colleges can play in their regional economies is that they are multipurpose institutions with multiple missions: they serve eighteen-year-olds seeking a low-cost way to get the first two years of a four-year degree, adults seeking basic literacy skills, workers whose jobs have disappeared and who need reskilling, and retirees seeking avocational learning opportunities. They are asked to serve these various constituencies on budgets that are typically substantially lower than those of regional four-year public colleges; in fact, a 2020 report from the Center for American Progress estimates that this funding gap is about $78 billion nationally.[1]

SELECTING FIVE CASE STUDY COLLEGES

In late fall 2021, with support from a private foundation, we set out to identify a small set of community colleges that were exemplary on two related dimensions: they prioritize career advancement for all learners across all programs, credit and noncredit alike; and through their close partnerships with regional employers and programmatic alignment with regional labor market needs, they have positioned themselves to be key players in their regions' workforce and economic development ecosystems.

To identify these colleges, we relied on a mix of quantitative and qualitative data, as well as recommendations from respected colleagues in the field. Once we identified over a dozen candidate institutions, we sorted them by region, urban/suburban/rural, enrollment size, racial/ethnic composition, Pell Grant percentage, part-time/full-time split, industry focus, top fields of study, median household income, and credit/noncredit split. We then developed a set of metrics by which to assess them—including retention and graduation rates, median earnings ten years after entering, median earnings compared to earnings of high school graduates in the region, and the share of students moving up two or more income quintiles.

With these data in hand, we then set up hour-long interviews with leadership teams from seven colleges. We began by asking each president to situate their college in the regional economy: What are the major industries, and how do they work with industry leaders to ensure alignment of their programs with industry needs? We asked about student demographics, and the degree to which they reflected the demographics of the region. We asked about degree programs and the balance between academic and career-focused majors. We asked about career navigation systems and the supports students were given early on to make program decisions based at least in part on regional labor market information. We asked about noncredit programs and their role in the college. We asked about the administrative structure of the college, with a particular interest in whether they had an employer-facing unit and how it was staffed, as well as their organizational strategy for bridging the credit/ noncredit divide. Finally, we asked about their willingness to fully collaborate on the development of a case study by giving us access to relevant planning documents and opening doors for our case writer.

These interviews were extraordinarily instructive. We came away impressed by the thoughtfulness and openness of the presidents and their teams and by their willingness to partner with us on this project.

All seven colleges met our core selection criteria, but at the end of the day, based on a set of diversity criteria—size, region, demographics—we selected the following five colleges:

Lorain County Community College (LCCC)—Ohio
Mississippi Gulf Coast Community College (MGCCC)—Mississippi
Northern Virginia Community College (NOVA)—Virginia
Pima Community College (Pima)—Arizona
San Jacinto Community College (San Jac)—Texas

They are diverse across several dimensions. Three of these colleges (NOVA, Pima, and San Jac) serve a majority minority student population. Pima is urban; Lorain, NOVA, and San Jac are in major metro regions (Cleveland; Washington, DC; and Houston, respectively); and MGGCCC has urban, suburban, and rural campuses. Three of these colleges are large, the other two (LCCC and MGGCC) more typical in size. Their percentage of full-time students ranges from 67 (MGCCC) to 23 (Pima). They are not as regionally diverse as we would have liked—the Northeast is unrepresented, the Southwest over-represented—but on the quality dimensions we cared most about, we felt both Pima and San Jac were sufficiently distinctive institutions to merit inclusion.

DRAFTING THE CASES

Once we completed the selection process, we then recruited five stellar graduate students and assigned them each a case. As you can see from their short bios in the About the Editors and Contributors section at the end of the book, they came to this task with diverse and interesting backgrounds. Two had journalism backgrounds, and the other three had significant research experience. Our guidance to them was to think of this assignment as long-form journalism, not academic research, and to focus not only on *what* these institutions have done to support the career goals of their students and to position themselves as key players in their regional economies, but on *how* they have done it.

We asked them to be especially attentive to the internal policies and institutional practices that have undergirded the success of these colleges on the two dimensions we prioritized, and we asked them to interview key business and community partners as well as key college leaders.[2]

Needless to say, these cases could not have been written on a three-month timeline, especially by students with full course loads, without the full cooperation of college leadership. Each president assigned someone on the senior leadership team to serve as the point of contact for our case writers. These contact points pulled together strategic planning and other relevant background documents, sent introductory notes to all prospective interviewees, and helped with the scheduling. At the end of the process, they carefully reviewed final drafts for accuracy to make sure we had the most current data and information. Their work is gratefully acknowledged at the end of this volume.

INTENDED AUDIENCES

From the beginning, we've had two primary audiences in mind for these cases. First, of course, are leaders from other colleges interested in strengthening the workforce side of their mission. Equally important, however, are governmental and business leaders in states that historically have not viewed or funded their community colleges as potential economic engines of regional development. Consequently, we recruited cross-sector leadership teams from six states—California, Colorado, Connecticut, Massachusetts, Minnesota, and New Jersey—and brought them together with the leaders of the case study colleges for a one-day virtual meeting on June 28, 2022, to explore the implications of these cases for their own states. You can find a recording of the June 28 convening on the Project on Workforce website, along with short videos we partnered to create featuring Lorain and Pima Community Colleges.[3]

CHAPTER 1

The Community's College

How Lorain County Community College
Drives Growth for Northeast Ohio

Hayley Glatter

EXECUTIVE SUMMARY

Straddling Lake Erie, Lorain County and Northeast Ohio sit at the epicenter of the American Rust Belt. The story of Lorain County Community College (LCCC) is both emblematic of the economic history of its region and also a harbinger of its future. In the 1960s, the college was founded as a hub to train workers for middle-skill jobs in automotive and steel. And at present, the college is absolutely integral to the region's ability to capitalize on the opportunities of the future: the transition to high-tech, high-skilled manufacturing, new investments in the semiconductor industry, the national movement toward insourcing, and the diversification of the regional economy through fields like healthcare and information technology (IT).

LCCC has a long-established reputation as the community's college. Externally, college leaders are viewed as stalwarts in the region. "Everyone knows LCCC" is a common refrain among Chamber of Commerce officials, industry organizations, and local officials. The college is proactive about reaching out to community organizations and engaging them as partners in grant competitions, serving on boards of directors, and leveraging local labor marketing data to build and scale programs that meet economic needs. The college's strategic planning process intentionally engages a wide variety of local stakeholders to inform its vision, ranging from K–12 leaders, parents, and four-year transfer partners to employers, faith-based organizations, and union leaders. In addition, over three thousand Lorain County high school students participate in dual enrollment at LCCC each term, embedding the college deeply into the local public school system.

Internally, LCCC has taken a "whole-college" approach to career services, engaging faculty and staff from across functional areas in workforce development. Through its Career by Design training sessions and an innovative badging series for advisors, LCCC is trying to ensure that every employee on campus can direct students to the information they need about job opportunities. The college has also engaged in curricular redesign to better expose students to career skills. LCCC's programs aim to front-load career information into coursework—whether it be bringing career guidance into the First-Year Experience curriculum, moving general education requirements to the backend of applied programs, or using dual enrollment to bring exposure to fields like IT earlier in the student life cycle.

As the local manufacturing industry contends with workforce shortages, LCCC is working actively to fill the gaps caused by both the Great Resignation and the longer-term challenges of an impending retirement wave. This includes efforts to reduce community-wide stigma around manufacturing and recruit diverse populations to the college. College leaders are vigorously involved in informational and advising interventions to show that the high-tech, knowledge-driven roles that exist today in advanced manufacturing are meaningfully different from the factory jobs that left past residents of Lorain County unemployed. LCCC has built innovative manufacturing programs complete with state-of-the-art on-campus facilities to reflect the reality that the future of manufacturing looks less like a factory and more like a lab.

In addition, the college is responsive to the needs of a changing student population. In recent years, the college has leaned into building new models that prioritize the needs of the working learner. LCCC has focused on scaling earn-and-learn models to new fields like automation and software development, understanding that many of the students it serves aim to avoid leaving the labor market, instead opting to earn credits and a paycheck simultaneously. Earn-and-learn students have block schedules to avoid class and work conflicts. Meanwhile, companies with real-time hiring needs are able to get access to the workers they need more quickly. In addition, during the COVID-19 pandemic, LCCC accelerated the growth of its fast-track training, which now spans sixty-five programs. The college specifically targeted recruitment of dislocated workers for free programs that run for sixteen weeks or less.

Finally, campus leaders are committed to ensuring that the new economic era does not leave behind precisely those residents who were hurt the most by past downturns. LCCC President Marcia Ballinger and her team are prioritizing equity across the institution. The school is leveraging data to identify fields and programs where students of color are under- or overrepresented.

TABLE 1.1 Lorain County Community College quick facts

Location	Cleveland-Elyria, OH (Urban, Midwest region)
Percentage of county residents who hold a bachelor's degree or above	25.3%
Median household income of county residents	$58,798
Total unduplicated enrollment count of credit and noncredit students	14,322
Percentage credit vs. noncredit	90% credit/10% noncredit
Percentage of full-time vs. part-time students (credit students only)	23% full-time/77% part-time
Percentage of students who received Pell Grants (credit students only)	53%
Percentage of students from the bottom 40% of the income distribution (credit students only)	31%

Sources: College Scorecard, 2021; US Department of Commerce Economics and Statistics Administration, US Census Bureau, US Department of Housing and Urban Development; US Census Bureau, 2020; Lorain County Community College; Raj Chetty, John Friedman, Emmanuel Saez, Nicholas Turner, and Danny Yagan, Mobility Report Cards: The Role of Colleges in Intergenerational Mobility, NBER Working Paper No. 23618, 2017.

FIGURE 1.1 LCCC enrollment by race/ethnicity, 2021–2022 academic year

FIGURE 1.2 LCCC enrollment by gender, 2021–2022 academic year

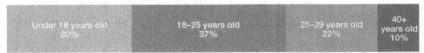

FIGURE 1.3 LCCC students by enrollment type (credit only), 2021–2022 academic year

| First-time college students 14% | Returning/continuing students 46% | Transfer students 7% | High school dual enrollment students 33% |

FIGURE 1.4 LCCC enrollment by age, 2021–2022 academic year*

| Under 18 years old 30% | 18–25 years old 37% | 25–39 years old 22% | 40+ years old 10% |

*LCCC does not capture age for all noncredit students due to personal identification information. This age distribution is reflective of all of the credit students and the 932 (out of 1,485) noncredit students whose ages are captured because they are enrolled in specific noncredit programs at LCCC.

INTRODUCTION

Like many community colleges, Lorain County Community College serves a diverse population of learners. Students in the Western outskirts of Cleveland look to LCCC to earn college credits while they are in high school, complete a valuable credential before transferring to a four-year institution, and upskill after decades in the workforce. But what makes LCCC unique is that beyond being a community college, leaders on campus have positioned the school as *the community's* college. A spirit of unity undergirds much of LCCC's work, as campus leaders are proactive about engaging internal and external partners in building manufacturing, healthcare, and IT programs that will effectively prepare students for the future of work.

LCCC is also contending with a community-wide stigma around manufacturing. The Rust Belt economy is synonymous with manufacturing, but in the last thirty years, factories have shuttered, companies have laid off scores of employees, and the national narrative around the future of American-made goods has been a lot of doom and gloom. LCCC cannot change any of that. The college cannot give students' parents their old jobs back or single-handedly reignite a new golden age of manufacturing in Ohio. But leaders at LCCC are adamant that this pessimistic view does not capture reality: domestic manufacturing is not some dirty, dying dinosaur; it is simply changing to look less like a factory and more like a lab. LCCC has built innovative career-centric manufacturing programs complete with state-of-the-art on-campus facilities to effectively prepare students for stable local jobs. These high-tech, knowledge-driven roles are meaningfully different from the factory jobs that left Lorain residents unemployed, and the school is making strides in convincing the community of this reality.

As manufacturing endures a wave of retirements among its aging employee population, LCCC is working to ensure its graduates are poised to fill the new roles that will drive local industry. And campus leaders are emphatic that equity is at the core of its mission, as they aim to bring its entire community along to the next phase of Cleveland's economic evolution.

A LOOK INSIDE LCCC AND THE RUST BELT

Profiling Northeast Ohio

Roughly 315,600 people call Lorain County, Ohio, home. Thirty miles west of Cleveland, Lorain is geographically diverse, encompassing industrial cities, like Elyria and Lorain, and farming communities, like Wellington and Penfield. Lorain's educational and socioeconomic profiles are similar to national averages: county residents have slightly higher high school attainment (90 percent versus 88.5 percent) and slightly lower bachelor's degree attainment (25.3 percent versus 32.9 percent) than the nation writ large. The median household income in Lorain County is $58,798, which is just below the national average of $64,994. Finally, the county is whiter than the nation as a whole—77.7 percent of Lorain residents identify as white, compared to 60.1 percent of the country overall, and Hispanic (10.4 percent versus 18.5 percent) and Black (9 percent versus 13.4 percent) people are underrepresented in Lorain.[1]

Lorain is also part of the broader Northeast Ohio region, which is home to about four million residents. Anchored by the cities of Cleveland and Akron, the region has a long history of manufacturing, and metro-Cleveland has served as a hub of American industry since the 1800s. Ohio factories have mass produced everything from clothes and farming equipment to sewing machines and paint. And beyond everyday consumer products, Cleveland made its name as the home of the iron industry.[2] By the early nineteenth century, and made all the more important by the demands of the Civil War, Ohio manufacturers made steam engines, trains, and other products crucial to the infrastructure of the industrial United States. The Cleveland Board of Trade estimates that by 1844, the 147 steel and iron manufacturers in the city produced goods worth $25.2 million and employed 14,000 people—but the region's industrial heyday didn't last forever. Between 1990 and 2018, Ohio lost almost four hundred thousand manufacturing jobs, and some residents still feel the sting of a legacy industry closing its plants and laying off its workforce.[3]

But manufacturing isn't dead in Northeast Ohio. It's different.

Today, manufacturing is a $46 billion industry in the region, accounting for roughly 20 percent of Northeast Ohio's GDP.[4] The eighteen-county area is home to 248,000 manufacturing workers employed by seven thousand companies—almost four hundred of which are in Lorain County specifically. These machinists, welders, inspectors, and mechanics make the products that keep society humming. What's more, the manufacturing industry is facing a wave of retirements among its skilled workforce[5] and, due in part to the negative stigma around the industry in Northeast Ohio, employers are struggling to hire talent to fill newly open roles. The domestic manufacturing sector, which is projected to grow by 4.1 percent in 2022, also faces supply chain challenges and cybersecurity vulnerabilities that could threaten its recovery from the pandemic.[6]

But manufacturing is not the only industry employing people in Northeast Ohio. Metro-Cleveland's healthcare and biomedical workforce swelled by 21 percent from 2001 to 2019 and now employs 270,000 people,[7] and the area's logistics and supply chain industry employs fifty-three thousand Ohioans.[8] Further, big companies are betting on Ohio. In January 2022, Intel announced it would invest more than $20 billion to build two chip factories outside of Columbus, creating ten thousand jobs by 2025.[9] The Intel investment is a signal that, despite the doom-and-gloom narratives about Rust Belt manufacturing, the industry—and Ohio's critical place in it—is still a major part of the local economy.

TABLE 1.2 Northeast Ohio's largest economic sectors by employment

Sector	Number of employees
Healthcare/biotech	270,000
Manufacturing	248,000
Professional services	187,000
Metal production and fabrication	106,000
Financial services	60,000
Logistics and supply chain	53,000
Aviation	37,000
Information technology	28,000
Automotive	26,000
Polymers and materials	26,000
Food processing	23,000

Source: Team NEO

Despite being a two-hour drive from the new Intel factories, officials at LCCC believe this investment will have a ripple effect throughout the entire state, creating meaningful opportunities for its students to make a difference: "We've been preparing for this moment," said Tracy Green, vice president of strategic and institutional development. "We know there's a big role for us as a community college to not only respond to community needs but also to have the foresight to understand where the hockey puck is going."

For now, that hockey puck appears to be headed straight for advanced manufacturing.

A Legacy Institution with Eyes on the Future

From the beginning, Lorain County Community College was built as a workforce incubator. LCCC opened its doors in 1963 as Ohio's first chartered community college with a permanent campus. At the time, automotive manufacturers were struggling to find middle-skill technicians to work at their steel plants, and LCCC emerged to fill the gap. Today, the college offers 203 degree and certificate programs in, among other fields, health and wellness, computer and information technologies, and, of course, engineering and manufacturing. Because LCCC does not receive as much state funding for noncredit programs, the vast majority—roughly 95 percent—of the school's programs are for credit, meaning students take classes that build toward a credential. Without state support, LCCC would have to pass the cost of the credential onto the student, which the college is very hesitant to do.

During the 2021–2022 academic year, Lorain enrolled 14,322 students, 23 percent full-time and 77 percent part-time. LCCC's student body is overwhelmingly female (61 percent versus 37 percent); white (69 percent, with 10 percent of students identifying as Hispanic/Latinx and 11 percent identifying as Black); and age twenty-four or below (67 percent versus 33 percent). Eighty-two percent of LCCC students received some kind of financial aid during the 2019–2020 school year, half of whom received Pell Grants and 44 percent of whom received grants from LCCC itself. The 9 percent of LCCC students who took out loans to attend college received an average of $3,856, primarily from the federal government.

In 2019, LCCC published a bold strategic plan called Vision 2025, outlining the institution's next five years.[10] The plan has five key focus areas, including increasing completion and academic success and improving the region's economic competitiveness. The plan was written before the pandemic upended not only LCCC's academic operations, but also Northeast Ohio's economic landscape. The college is wrestling with four key workforce development challenges as it looks to the next phase of its history, which this case study describes in detail:

1. Overcoming negative stereotypes about manufacturing
2. Front-loading curricula so that students get the skills they need sooner and can start working
3. Navigating Ohio's complex funding structure, which supports only credit-seeking students
4. Recruiting students as high school enrollments decline and demand for workers increases among a wave of pandemic-related retirements.

THE LCCC APPROACH
Reducing Silos

In many parts of the country, community colleges are bifurcated between credit and noncredit programs. When these functions are especially divided, colleges operate on the assumption that students are either working toward a bachelor's degree or working toward work itself; for both groups, community college is a means to an end, but members of the former use their time on campus as a springboard to even higher education, while the latter is focused on upskilling or reskilling for a specific profession. LCCC perceives this distinction as completely artificial: "Economic development, workforce development, and academic programming go hand in hand," Dean of Engineering Technologies Kelly Zelesnik said. "At some point, our students are going to be seeking gainful employment—whether they transfer or not."

Some students who start at LCCC may go on to be career academics, transferring to get their bachelor's degree before pursuing a master's degree and a PhD. But even those long-term students will someday be part of the workforce. And rather than keeping transfer and workforce programs and students separate, the school has taken a more holistic approach to transfer education, aiming to teach students who aspire to get their bachelors' degrees the skills they need to be successful employees.

LCCC operationalizes this ethos through the *guided pathways framework*, a structured approach that encourages students to navigate the community college with an end career or educational goal in mind.[11] It leverages meta-majors to organize fields of study into broad career sectors and assist students in working backward to design a course load that helps them achieve their aspirations. Crucially, however, LCCC personnel encourage students to take their academics and careers one step at a time, really considering how much education an individual needs to do the type of work that they want. The school aims to be a touchpoint for students throughout their working and educational lives, whether it's for a two-year associate degree, a series of certificates over the course of a decade, or any flight pattern in between. "We have a

> "At some point, our students are going to be seeking gainful employment—whether they transfer or not."
> —Kelly Zelesnik, Dean of Engineering Technologies

> "There's nobody in Lorain that doesn't know LCCC. People know that if they want training, that's exactly where they should go."
> —*Ethan Karp, President of the Manufacturing Extension Partnership (MAGNET)*

great appreciation for how the greater ecosystem works," LCCC President Marcia Ballinger said. "We're not in isolation as the community college where people come and take classes and leave. We are vested in their future."

Part of that investment is in building relationships with students and ensuring that every adult on campus can be a valuable career resource able to communicate the long-term career options that will be available to students depending on the path they take. As such, teams from across the college—including advisors, career services, business growth services, and financial aid—all participate in guided pathways programming.[12] They are taught to consider the student's individual goals, talents, and interests so that they can help put each student on a track toward a fulfilling career that will earn them a family-sustaining wage.

The Community's College

"There's nobody in Northeast Ohio that doesn't know LCCC," said Ethan Karp, the president of the Manufacturing Extension Partnership (MAGNET). "People know that if they want training, that's exactly where they should go."

LCCC is an anchor of its community. President Ballinger and her staff are committed to raising educational attainment in Northeast Ohio and moving their neighbors toward economic prosperity. They see the college as a critical part of the regional ecosystem and have built strong relationships with individual employers, local leaders, and industry associations to ensure they have the information they need to build programs that prepare students to fill the gaps in the college's community partners' workforces.

"Lorain County has been through a lot of ups and downs as far as businesses closing, moving, and consolidating," said Tony Gallo, the president of the Lorain County Chamber of Commerce. "Lorain County Community College has always been there to say, 'Okay, that was really bad. What do we do to move forward to get past this?'"

THE COMMUNITY'S CONNECTOR

LCCC views employers and workforce leaders as critical partners in achieving its long-term vision. As part of the strategic planning process that began in 2018, the college engaged K–12 stakeholders, university partners, employers, and other constituents—including faith-based organizations and union leaders. This work culminated in 2019 with LCCC's Vision 2025 report, which outlines objectives and key results for how the college can help create a more vibrant, equitable community. The key objectives of Vision 2025 are as follows:[13]

1. Expand participation in LCCC programs among working-age adults and K–12 learners.
2. Increase completion and academic success via expanded programmatic offerings, university and employer partnerships, and student supports.
3. Foster student success through more work-based learning opportunities and connections to in-demand jobs.
4. Improve economic competitiveness through a deliberate focus on skills, entrepreneurship, and innovation.
5. Enhance everyone's quality of life by serving as a convener and broad-based community resource.

The plan is refreshed every year, and the college relies on regular environmental scans and surveys to assess its next steps and ensure it is capable of matching the local economic opportunity with various programmatic offerings.

Another way LCCC keeps its finger on the pulse of local economic development and serves as a community connector is by housing an Ohio Small Business Development Center (SBDC).[14] The statewide SBDC system supports small companies by providing no-cost advising, access to capital, educational training, and more to entrepreneurs at various stages of the business development process. The businesses that leverage SBDC services create jobs in Lorain County and, being in close proximity to LCCC staff and faculty, facilitate information sharing and relationship building that the college can use to ensure their graduates are the ones filling those new roles.[15] "We are the convener," President Ballinger said. "We are the common ground that can bring the stakeholders together. We're the community solution provider."

ASSESSING LABOR MARKET NEEDS

LCCC relies on a variety of qualitative and quantitative data sources to assess local labor market needs. It then operationalizes these data into programmatic offerings. The college relies on information from Lightcast (formerly Emsi Burning Glass), a premier labor market analytics firm, to model labor market data and to get a sense of the job titles that employers are hiring for. The college also works with Team NEO, a Northeast Ohio regional economic development hub, to get additional data on workforce needs. President Ballinger sits on Team NEO's board and cochairs the Talent Development Council.[16] By engaging with Team NEO in both high-touch and low-touch ways, LCCC officials can more efficiently connect their students with open jobs.

LCCC officials also stay heavily involved in various affinity groups and professional organizations in the community to gather labor market information. For example, President Ballinger sits on the board of the Lorain County Chamber of Commerce and attends its annual economic summit. This meeting allows for essential information exchange: not only does President Ballinger maintain and build new relationships with specific employers, but she also informs businesses about what's happening at the college and how companies can take advantage of LCCC's resources.[17]

Further, LCCC has formal partners with healthcare, IT, and manufacturing groups. The school is proactive about reaching out to organizations like MAGNET, which supports manufacturers in the region.[18] Rather than serving exclusively as a thought partner, LCCC in the past has also identified funding opportunities for manufacturing start-ups and brought MAGNET into federal grant proposals for talent planning. For example, Ballinger led the collaboration between businesses and colleges, linking the two as MAGNET worked on a Build Back Better grant focused on increasing the diversity of students in STEM programs.[19] There are shared personnel between MAGNET and LCCC, which strengthens the bond and flow of information between the two.

"They're the MVP that provides us education technical assistance," MAGNET's Ethan Karp said. "There's often a lot of really good overlap where our companies can benefit from them and vice versa."

CURRICULAR DESIGN WITH EMPLOYER INPUT

Many community colleges struggle to form meaningful relationships with employers. However, LCCC has thrived. The college engages employers deeply in the curricular design process to ensure it is preparing students with the skills they need to compete in the modern labor market and fill the hiring gaps of local companies. The college is dedicated to listening to employers and is transitioning from a faculty-driven to an industry-driven curricular design model. The college launched peer-to-peer faculty conversations to ensure that all faculty members—including those who may be hesitant to substitute employers' plans for their own teaching strategies—have their voices heard and are engaged in this work.[20] LCCC is also considering launching listening training sessions with an executive in residence to further formalize its push to incorporate employer feedback.

The school also engages employers to serve on advisory committees when they are building new programs or updating old ones, and faculty members work with program developers to canvas the industry and find experts who might be interested in participating in an advisory role.[21] This work flowed from a National Science Foundation–funded project to the Center for Occupational Research and Development, which focused on building strong advisory committees.[22] Ultimately, LCCC hopes to listen and respond to industry skill needs, rather than tell industries what students are prepared to do. And, in some cases, LCCC is forging design and delivery partnerships with industry partners, building apprenticeship programs and then requesting that professionals serve as adjunct faculty; not only does this ensure students are learning from experts with up-to-date knowledge and experiences, but it also helps LCCC shore up its shortage of qualified instructors.[23]

On top of curricular design, part of engaging employers more deeply involves matching their goals to various programmatic offerings and balancing those goals with what students need. LCCC is spinning out more earn-and-learn programs, which allow students to simultaneously earn credits and be on the job. For example, after a cyber company came to LCCC looking for one hundred skilled people as soon as possible, the college placed student interns with the firm and began developing a security operation center on campus that allows them to train future learners on industry-standard equipment.[24]

LCCC knows that the labor market and skill demands evolve quickly. The school conducts program evaluations examining enrollment and labor market information once every three years to determine whether it is preparing students to fill an actual economic need. These thorough reviews include feedback from employers and alumni and incorporate salary data, an important metric for ensuring LCCC is fulfilling its equity mission and serving as an engine of economic opportunity. Officials at LCCC rely on this information—combined with early momentum metrics that predict graduation and further academic achievement—to determine whether to sunset or scale programs.[25]

Redesigning Career Advising

A THOUGHTFUL APPROACH TO MATCHING STUDENTS
TO OPPORTUNITY

From 2011 to 2016, LCCC participated in the Gates Foundation–funded Completion by Design initiative, which aimed to increase the number of low-income adults who earned postsecondary credentials and decrease the time it took them to do so.[26] Completion by Design left a strong legacy at LCCC and gave faculty, staff, and leadership experience with getting campus-wide buy-in on specific initiatives. The program also clarified the need to leverage data, consider a student's broader path, and think through how the college can assist students in moving forward.

Out of this experience, LCCC's Career by Design was born. The initiative constitutes a reframing of the student journey and end goal, embedding career advising and aspirations from the very beginning.[27] This philosophy prompts students to think about how they envision their postschool lives and careers and to consider what types of jobs are available now and in the future that allow them to have and earn a living wage. Career by Design is a framework that can be applied to students of any age and at any point in their educational career, and LCCC officials see it as a way to benchmark the value of the credentials they're providing and hold themselves accountable.

"The goal is to get people connected to the college at a starting point where they can continue to grow and to make sure that, campus-wide, not only is there buy-in but there's knowledge," said Cindy Kushner, the director of school and community partnerships. "Faculty and staff should be able to talk competently about career services so students feel they can trust us and that they're making good choices for themselves and their families."

STRATEGIES FOR OPERATIONALIZATION

LCCC has implemented its Career by Design philosophy through a variety of internal, staff-centric programs, as well as student-facing curricular reforms. These efforts include the following:

- *Badging series:*[28] A core piece of Career by Design requires all adults on campus to be able to serve as effective career resources for students. For them to do so, staff need to have a sense of local labor market trends and employer needs. With this in mind, LCCC launched a badging series for advisors and career services personnel to ensure they're empowered with the information they need to help students make informed career decisions. Over the course of a series of five trainings delivered by LCCC and its regional economic development partners, career counselors and advisors learned about local labor needs, as well as what contemporary roles entail. Of the seventy-one outreach, advising, and career staff who attended the workshops, forty-one went through the entire series, completed a culminating assessment, and earned a certificate from the college.
- *First-year experience course:*[29] LCCC redesigned its first-year experience course to front-load career-related information. The updated version presents students with information about Northeast Ohio's economic landscape. Students also research a field they are interested in and then articulate in journal entries and conversations with instructors whether, based on what they learned, they think they might (or might not) be a good fit for a particular job. Not only does this assignment give students an opportunity to learn more about what's out there, but it also allows both students and faculty to unearth and debunk some of the myths students have around certain jobs—especially around manufacturing. LCCC used a Title III grant to complete the curricular redesign so that it was more palatable for adult learners.
- *Focus on dual enrollment:* Dual enrollment programs allow high school students to earn college credits at a local community college before they finish twelfth grade. Historically, the programs targeted high achievers interested in getting a jump on an associate's degree, but at LCCC,

leaders see dual enrollment as an opportunity to reach underrepresented students and expose them to college early.[30] Dual enrollment is available to Ohio students starting in seventh grade, and over three thousand dual enrollment students take classes at LCCC each term. The college ensures that these younger students spend time thinking about their future careers while on campus and set up meetings with a college and career advisor who can direct them toward other programs at LCCC that they might be a good fit for. LCCC's College Credit Plus program, for example, focuses on introducing dual enrollment students to computer science and other core technical programs that they may not have been aware of previously.[31] This program ideally serves as a gateway to other LCCC career programs, helping students build momentum toward a meaningful credential.

- *Emphasis on short-term training:* To fill employer needs as efficiently as possible, LCCC restructured programs to give students the minimum skills they need to get to work as soon as possible. "They're getting front-loaded with some of those work skills that are in demand, then they get to work while they build, grow, and apply those skills immediately," Kushner said. Front-loading skills, Kushner said, can be an effective way to get adult learners who may not have any experience in college engaged in their learning because the lessons feel valuable from the start. The Building IT Futures program, for example, aims to be a launching pad for students into computer science. The program engages high school dual enrollment students and allows them to take courses in microcomputer applications, database design and implementation, and programming before they finish twelfth grade.[32] Then, if those students enroll in LCCC after high school, they will have credits toward a computer science degree, which falls under the college's computers and IT pathway. LCCC's short-term programs are also designed with equity in mind. The school leverages data from Team NEO to identify programs where students of color are under- or overrepresented and offers sixty-five programs that run for sixteen weeks or less free of charge.[33] The majority of these "fast-track programs," which were started via a Department of Education grant and sustained through LCCC's braided funding approach, are in manufacturing, IT, and healthcare.[34] They attract more diverse students than the general LCCC population (40 percent of enrollees are students of color),[35] and the credentials students attain can be terminal or serve as a springboard for additional learning.[36]

- *Building earn-and-learn programs:* LCCC's Train Ohio program allows full-time students to split their time, spending two days a week in the classroom and three days a week working for a sponsor company.[37] These students are paid for their work, gaining valuable on-the-job experience and building relationships with professionals in their areas of interest.[38] Companies, meanwhile, get the workers they need quickly. LCCC offers earn-and-learn opportunities in five fields, including software development and automation engineering, and is looking to expand these applied programs. Further, earn-and-learn programs aim to be responsive to the preexisting talent pool, recognizing that many automation students are incumbent workers looking to upskill. As such, this model allows learners to avoid a potential discontinuity in their career and instead earn credits and a paycheck simultaneously. Train Ohio participants have block schedules to avoid class and work conflicts, and they have the chance to shadow employers, participate in mock interviews, and refine their resumes.[39] LCCC also gathers data from participating companies to monitor student progress. Train Ohio team members are in contact with employers' human resources managers to get a sense of how well LCCC is preparing students and whether there are gaps the school could fill more effectively.

THE FUTURE OF MANUFACTURING

The assembly line manufacturing of the American Rust Belt anchored both the regional economy and national supply chain throughout the nineteenth and twentieth centuries. In Lorain County, families passed jobs from one generation to the next in a local automotive factory or steel plant, simultaneously building American-made products and a legacy of gritty hard work. The Rust Belt was home to about half of the country's manufacturing workers in 1950 and, before 1980, the region's auto, steel, and rubber makers had as much as a 90 percent market share.[40] But as competition grew, unions were weakened, and talent moved elsewhere, Rust Belt manufacturing declined. In fact, between 2000 and 2010, the Midwest lost 1.6 million manufacturing jobs as the sector's labor force shrunk by 35 percent.[41] This evolution has been painful for families across LCCC's service region, and officials there know that they have to combat manufacturing's negative stereotypes. "We're struggling in manufacturing because it doesn't have the best reputation," Kushner said. "Even though it doesn't look like it used to, you still have Grandpa and Grandma telling stories about their bad experiences."

LCCC's industry partners also recognize the power that manufacturing's legacy holds over the community. "When you say to a student, 'You can be a nurse, you can be an IT professional, or you can be a manufacturer,' I think the other jobs sound sexier," Karp said. "People understand them better and they understand their career progression better. Manufacturing is stigmatized as being an unstable career since people have seen so many people be laid off from it."

The State of Modern Manufacturing

But today, manufacturing isn't the dark, dirty, dangerous work that it was seventy-five years ago. Now LCCC is preparing its students to work with robots in clean rooms, which are isolated from contamination and frequently used for industrial production and scientific research. These skilled workers will operate sophisticated technology and produce microchips, circuit boards, and other electronics. The scale of manufacturing in Northeast Ohio is roughly the same today as it was in the 1960s and 1970s, but, due to automation, the sector now employs fewer people who can do a higher volume of work. Wages have broadly kept pace with inflation, as the average nonsupervisory manufacturing employee earned about seven dollars an hour in 1980 and earns about twenty-four dollars an hour today.[42]

The manufacturing sector is also experiencing a so-called silver tsunami as skilled workers retire and exit the workforce; 2.5 million manufacturing jobs are expected to open between 2020 and 2030 as a result of this wave of retirements.[43] As companies look to fill these roles with new employees, they are looking for workers with both hard and soft skills, including literacy, numeracy, and critical thinking. However, so far, manufacturers are struggling to find qualified talent, and some estimates suggest that half of the projected four million manufacturing jobs to be created between 2020 and 2030 will be difficult to fill.[44] "The thing manufacturers want most is the trained person,"

Karp said. "If you have a steady flow of trained people, the manufacturers would have unending demand."

LCCC is at the forefront of training the community to fill these jobs. In addition to its programmatic offerings, the school is embedded in the manufacturing industry at the local, regional, and state level: locally, the college serves as the fiscal agent for the Lorain County Manufacturing Partnership; regionally, President Ballinger sits on the board of MAGNET; and LCCC is the facilitator of the statewide Ohio TechNet consortium, which is devoted to remedying the manufacturing sector's workforce shortage.[45]

SPOTLIGHT ON MICROELECTROMECHANICAL SYSTEMS

LCCC says it is being proactive about preparing its students for the future of manufacturing. This effort is exemplified by the school's microelectromechanical systems (MEMS) program, which trains students in areas like soldering, computer skills, mechanical drafting, and electronics. These students could help solve America's microchip shortage,[46] going to work for companies like Quality Electrodynamics, which makes the electronics that support the MRI equipment Phillips provides to hospitals.[47]

The MEMS program is conducted in conjunction with eighty industry partners. In 2018, it became Ohio's first community college–based bachelor's degree program because LCCC had employer support and was not duplicating a preexisting university program. Students interested in MEMS can pursue a bachelor's degree, associate's degree, one-year certificate, or half-year certificate, which front-loads specific skills and requires fewer general education classes.[48]

The program, which enrolls about thirty-six students per year and costs roughly $4,000 a year for a full-time student, includes a suite of work-based learning opportunities and gives students access to state-of-the-art equipment on campus. Some MEMS partner companies pay students around seventeen dollars an hour, allowing students to earn enough to pay for a significant portion of their tuition. For example, Libra Industries, an Ohio-based systems integrator, has agreed to cover the cost of the associate's and bachelor's degrees for LCCC students working at least twenty hours a week. MEMS has a 100 percent postgraduation employment rate, and more than 85 percent of enrolled students have part-time internships or full-time jobs.[49] In the past,

MEMS students have been hired full time by the companies they intern for after they finish the program.

LCCC first learned about the need for MEMS in 2012, when officials began hearing from local circuit board and chip companies—including one that participated in the on-campus small business incubator—about its workforce gaps.[50] In 2013, the school began building its hands-on, training-centric degree. LCCC secured industry support, which made it eligible for the state funding it needed to purchase equipment. Supportive companies agreed to sign on to the program in exchange for LCCC placing student interns there. Like all of LCCC's credit programs, MEMS is funded through state-share instruction, so when a student completes a course or earns a degree, Ohio pays LCCC to keep the program alive. Because the majority of funding is based on students graduating, the program's viability is largely determined by workforce outcomes, so MEMS faculty are highly incentivized to work closely with companies in the field. "Our eighty industry partners tell us what we should be teaching people, because if we're not training a student in a particular skill, then they don't get a job, and I don't have a degree to teach," MEMS Program Coordinator Johnny Vanderford said.

One distinctive feature of LCCC's MEMS program is that the college, through federal, state, and philanthropic support, built a $1.5 million state-of-the-art facility to train students in advanced manufacturing skills. According to Vanderford, access to the same equipment as some of the major companies in the area gives students the hands-on experience they need to be successful at work in the safe learning environment of school. Further, having the equipment and the wage-subsidized degree helps destigmatize the community college experience by making the labor market benefits of the program more immediate. LCCC allows other universities and companies to use its lab for training institutes, and students have the chance to visit the facility in the evenings, which is especially helpful for those participating in more theory-heavy programs that may provide fewer practical opportunities.

Vanderford and his colleagues say they rely on company feedback to help make decisions about topics like what equipment to buy and what skills students need to acquire as soon as possible. LCCC has three major mechanisms for gathering this feedback:

1. *Communication around work-based learning:* LCCC instructors are required to check in with students and employers every week, and students write reports on their internship experiences. Supervisor feedback also affects students' grades in the course. This process allows the college to understand pain points and successes as they emerge.

2. *Hitting the job market:* Vanderford and his colleagues say they search for what companies are posting on LinkedIn, scan job boards and send listings to students, and constantly engage with alumni to understand how the field is evolving. LCCC looks for similarities in job descriptions to understand what is common across the industry and to ensure it is training students with skills that will not become obsolete. In exchange for LCCC connecting employers to students, it expects employers to tell them what they want workers to be trained to do.

3. *Participatory advisory committee:* The MEMS advisory committee meets a few times a year and includes engineers, technologists, manufacturers, and HR recruiters who share what their needs are. The advisory committee has unearthed valuable curricular and personnel insights for LCCC, including, for example, that people have to be smoke-free for six months to work in biomedical manufacturing and that some jobs require higher-level background checks than others.

AN INNOVATIVE FUNDING STRUCTURE

LCCC's leaders have worked to foster a culture of innovation and risk-taking that comes straight from the president's office. Ballinger and her colleagues are committed to avoiding complacency and pursuing creative partnerships and new opportunities. "This is an area that's known for innovation, invention, and being a little bit scrappy," said Marisa Vernon White, the vice president of enrollment management and student services. "We have blue-collar roots, and I think it shows up in how we work. We are very willing to roll up our sleeves and do what we need to make something happen."

> "This is an area that's known for innovation, invention, and being a little bit scrappy. We have blue-collar roots, and I think it shows up in how we work. We are very willing to roll up our sleeves and do what we need to make something happen."
>
> —Marisa Vernon White,
> Vice President of
> Enrollment Management
> and Student Services

This philosophy impacts the student experience in myriad ways—including, crucially, financial aid and program funding. LCCC has what it calls a *braided funding* model that includes state and local appropriations, as well as federal grants from several departments. LCCC is funded in part by a local tax levy, which leaders say keeps them accountable and responsive to the community.[51] In recent years, LCCC has also found increasing success in securing federal grants to pilot big projects but has strategically avoided becoming singularly reliant on one funding source. Terri Sandu's research and development team is 90 to 95 percent grant funded, and the college's Sponsored Programs Office manages the grants, acknowledging that doing so should not be an afterthought.[52] LCCC has received, among others, a grant from the Department of Defense, which is investing in manufacturing workforce development and its impact on the industrial defense supply chain,[53] as well as the Department of Labor, which provided $15 million to establish the Ohio TechNet consortium in 2014.[54] LCCC and ten other colleges in the state joined the initiative, which is focused on advanced manufacturing. Now, all twenty-three Ohio community colleges have joined, along with seven universities and twelve technical centers.

Rather than not trying something because there is not full funding to support the entire initiative, LCCC looks for sufficient funding to get a promising project off the ground, establish a proof of concept, and then seek additional support for scaling. The school maintains a dashboard with key performance indicators on student success and impact as determined by grant proposal deliverables to determine whether to sunset, pause, or scale various programs.

LCCC has leveraged this braided approach to circumvent Ohio's funding structure, which only supports credit-seeking students. LCCC leaders believe it is their responsibility to provide aid to all students who need it: "We've made a blanket statement and the promise that, particularly during the pandemic, if you want to take a fast-track program to get reemployed into a high-growth sector, we've got your back," said Tracy Green.

CONCLUSION

LCCC's story is emblematic of a college working to adapt to challenging economic trends outside of its control. The school leaders say they insist on giving everyone—students, faculty, and industry partners—the opportunity to try, and have created a supportive, data-driven environment to gather feedback and make decisions about whether those attempts are worth pursuing in the long term. Campus leaders have proven that they are willing to experiment by piloting new programs, like MEMS, and pursuing alternative strategies to support their students, like the Career by Design framework. This proactive approach is preparing students for the next generation of jobs that employers in Northeast Ohio are eager to fill. By front-loading skills in short-term credential programs and reimagining its employer partnerships, LCCC works to ensure that its students are prepared both efficiently and thoroughly.

At the heart of this work is LCCC's dedication to its community. Throughout the past decade, LCCC has opened its doors as a community provider to the people of Northeast Ohio. In the next decade, as the economy of Ohio reacts to the silver tsunami and changes within the manufacturing industry, LCCC will have to adapt to the needs of its people. One thing is clear: the college is ready to work with its community partners to address these issues together. In the meantime, it is up to the college to be responsive and capitalize on the opportunities of the future.

CHAPTER 2

"Everything We Do Is Workforce Training"

Why Mississippi Gulf Coast Community College Breaks Down Walls

Analisa Sorrells

EXECUTIVE SUMMARY

Amid an unprecedented level of voluntary exits from the workforce in the wake of the COVID-19 pandemic and a record-high number of job openings,[1] the traditional role of Mississippi Gulf Coast Community College (MGCCC) as a talent pipeline for South Mississippi is more important than ever. The college is redesigning education in a way that focuses on providing students with valuable skills and credentials needed to power the region's growth, regardless of their educational pathways. With the launch of its new strategic plan, Excelerate 2030, MGCCC codified specific strategies aimed to accomplish an ambitious mission over the next ten years.

Situated within a largely rural state with lower levels of educational attainment in the population, MGCCC is one of the most important players in the regional economy. Contending with a brain drain, long-standing structural inequities in its neighborhoods, and limited postsecondary education and training options, the college is at the center of efforts to build more pathways into good jobs in its four-county region. With strong partnerships across shipbuilding, energy and utilities, aerospace, healthcare, and tourism, the institution has a compelling track record to prove that community college credentials can provide accessible entry points into family-sustaining careers.

MGCCC's ambitious launch of its new schools model marks a near-complete overhaul of the college's organizational design, intentionally blurring the lines among academic courses, career and technical education (CTE), and noncredit training. Eight subject-based schools—uniting all of the college's offerings, both credit and noncredit—were created to provide a more flexible roadmap for students as they work toward a credential, be it a certificate, degree, or certification. The schools model collapses all of the college's former departments into one of eight topic-focused schools: business, law, hospitality, and culinary; engineering, mathematics, data science, and IT; manufacturing, maritime, and transportation; science and kinesiology; nursing and health professions; human sciences and education; language arts; and visual and performing arts.

One key component of MGCCC's approach is its deep investment in employer relationships. In its relationships with employers, MGCCC staff are focused on how to get to "yes." The college's president and other members of senior leadership are always present in conversations with local employers and set the tone for the school's focus on partnership. Within the college's organizational structure, noncredit and credit leadership work hand in hand to support employers' requests. Often in the first meetings with an employer, representatives from both types of programs show up to the table together to understand how to best meet the employers' needs, allowing them to answer questions and provide information up front to help employers identify the customized, best-fit option.

MGCCC understands the financial constraints facing many of its students and has put a premium on developing earn-and-learn models, in which students can be paid on the job as they learn new skills. MGCCC supports apprenticeship programs across six different employers, with programs ranging in size from small cohorts at Rolls Royce to cohorts of seventy-plus apprentices at Ingalls Shipbuilding. Its new pilot program in partnership with Singing River Health System represents the first licensed practical nurse

(LPN) apprenticeship in the state of Mississippi. MGCCC goes above and beyond the traditional role of a community college in developing new programs: in addition to listening to employers' needs and codesigning solutions, the college also assists in getting programs passed through necessary regulatory processes for state-level certifications.

To understand its success, MGCCC uses robust data analytics to analyze how its job-focused programs are performing and where improvements can be made. Through the use of thirteen health metrics, all fifty-six CTE programs are assigned an annual score, allowing the college's leadership to quickly understand where challenges and opportunities exist. The specificity of the data the college collects also results in actionable improvement plans that drill down into the specific areas with the biggest need for growth.

Finally, MGCCC has stepped up to address occupational segregation in its region's talent pipeline. Students of color are actually overrepresented relative to their population share in the surrounding four-county region, but the college knows it is on a continuing journey to advance equity. The robust nature of the college's data systems allows stakeholders to disaggregate and analyze program outcomes across variables such as age, gender, race and ethnicity, and socioeconomic status. College leadership is keenly focused on addressing demographic differences in program enrollment, especially when some groups of students are underrepresented in the programs with the highest wages. The college is rolling out targeted recruitment strategies for fields that have historically lacked diversity, as well as revamping its own hiring practices as an institution.

INTRODUCTION

When Dr. Mary Graham began working at Mississippi Gulf Coast Community College in the early 1990s, one of her first roles was as the workforce director. At that time, the college's workforce training efforts focused solely on noncredit contract training and building relationships with local business and industry. According to Graham, there weren't many private entities focused on workforce training, so the college worked to fill this void and began to establish its role as a workforce training leader in the region. One of MGCCC's first workforce training partnerships was with Ingalls Shipbuilding, a company that the college has been partnering with via an apprentice program since the 1950s. "We were going out and really trying to offer our services . . .

TABLE 2.1 Mississippi Gulf Coast Community College quick facts*

Location	Gulfport-Biloxi, MS (Rural, Southeast)
Percentage of county residents who hold a bachelor's degree or above	15.2%
Median household income of county residents	$47,683
Total unduplicated enrollment count of credit and non-credit students	20,282
Percentage credit vs. noncredit	56% credit/44% noncredit
Percentage of full-time vs. part-time students (credit students only)	41% full-time/ 59% part-time
Percentage of students who received Pell Grants (credit students only)	62%
Percentage of students from the bottom 40% of the income distribution (credit students only)	42%

Sources: College Scorecard, 2021; US Department of Commerce Economics and Statistics Administration, US Census Bureau, US Department of Housing and Urban Development; US Census Bureau, 2020; Mississippi Gulf Coast Community College; Raj Chetty, John Friedman, Emmanuel Saez, Nicholas Turner, and Danny Yagan, Mobility Report Cards: The Role of Colleges in Intergenerational Mobility, NBER Working Paper No. 23618, 2017.

*Enrollment data represents 2021–2022 numbers, inclusive of credit, noncredit, and dual enrollment students, as provided by Mississippi Gulf Coast Community College.

FIGURE 2.1 MGCCC enrollment by race/ethnicity, 2021–2022 academic year

FIGURE 2.2 MGCCC enrollment by gender, 2021–2022 academic year

FIGURE 2.3 MGCCC students by enrollment type (credit only), 2021–2022 academic year

FIGURE 2.4 MGCCC enrollment by age, 2021–2022 academic year

to a lot of business and industry, to let them know that we were in the business of workforce training and that we could do it in a flexible, responsive, creative way," said Graham.

Back then, Graham remembers there being a somewhat competitive internal spirit between the noncredit and credit sides of the college, especially when it came to things like sharing equipment and classroom space. Now, as president of the college, Graham says the relationship between credit and noncredit has transformed into a symbiotic one. "The culture at Gulf Coast has changed for us dramatically," she said. "It's been a great evolutionary process for the greater good for the institution and for business and industry."

But this didn't happen overnight. It was a slow shift over many years to bring the college to where it is today: there is now no distinction drawn between the college's credit and noncredit offerings. Instead, instruction at the college is called *teaching and learning*—and it is everything the college does.

"Everything we do is workforce training—whether you're on the academic track, the career and technical credit track, or the noncredit workforce track—everything is workforce training," said Graham.

WHO DOES MGCCC SERVE?

Mississippi Gulf Coast's roots began with the founding of the Harrison County Agricultural High School in 1911.[2] The school started operating in 1912 in Perkinston, located roughly thirty miles north of Gulfport, which sits on the Gulf of Mexico. In 1942, the final county joined the institution's four-county service area—George County, Jackson County, Stone County, and Harrison County. Since 1987, the college has operated as Mississippi Gulf Coast Community College. The college has three campuses—Perkinston, Jackson County, and Harrison County—and seven additional training centers.[3] Gulfport, located in Harrison County, is the second largest city in the state after Jackson, the capital.[4]

In a largely rural state with low educational attainment, high rates of poverty, and wide socioeconomic inequality, the role of community colleges in providing workforce training as a pathway to good jobs and economic mobility is imperative. As of 2020, Mississippi's poverty

> "Everything we do is workforce training—whether you're on the academic track, the career and technical credit track, or the noncredit workforce track—everything is workforce training."
> —*Dr. Mary Graham, President, Mississippi Gulf Coast Community College*

rate was 20.3 percent, the highest in the country.[5] From 2015 to 2019, only 22 percent of Mississippians ages twenty-five and older held a bachelor's degree, the second lowest educational attainment rate in the country.[6] And the state's wage gap between Black and white earners is one of the nation's largest, with Black women who work full-time and year-round earning fifty-six cents on the dollar compared to white, non-Hispanic men who do the same.[7]

This context makes the workforce training efforts of two-year institutions like Mississippi Gulf Coast all the more important. With a vast majority of the state's population not holding four-year college degrees, Mississippi's community colleges play a critical role in the economy's ability to thrive, ensuring that the workforce is equipped with high-value skills and credentials and that programs are flexible to meet employers' shifting workforce needs. From 2017 to 2018, 49 percent of students in Mississippi were enrolled in the state's fifteen public two-year colleges,[8] which is higher than the national average of 44 percent.[9]

Deeneaus Polk, an MGCCC alumnus, was born and raised in Pascagoula, Mississippi, a town of roughly twenty-two thousand people located along the coast in Jackson County.[10] He describes it as a blue-collar town with an economy fueled by major industries like Ingalls Shipbuilding and Chevron's oil refinery. "There's a real appreciation for work where I'm from," said Polk. "This town has always had a grit to it, and that grit has always been refined in a way by Mississippi Gulf Coast Community College. It's a place that has always sort of been ubiquitous throughout the community in regard to opportunity."

Although the state's total population declined slightly over the last decade, the college's region has experienced growth, along with an increased connectedness to the broader Gulf Coast region—from New Orleans, Louisiana, to the west to Mobile, Alabama, to the east. From 2010 to 2020, only eighteen of Mississippi's eighty-two counties experienced population growth, including all four counties in MGCCC's service area. Harrison County experienced an 11.5 percent increase in population, one of the highest rates of growth in the state.[11]

Along with that growth has come demographic shifts, including growing communities of color. Between the 2013–2014 and 2018–2019 school years, the number of associate's degrees earned by Black and Hispanic graduates in Mississippi increased by 19 percent.[12]

According to Polk, the shifting socioeconomic status of the region, coupled with the fact that cities in nearby states may offer more competitive wages, creates the threat of brain drain—people moving away from Mississippi's Gulf coast and, in many cases, never coming back. "The question really becomes, If this is what it's always been, what are we going to become in the future to ensure that those who do remain want to stay here and know that they have a viable future for both themselves and their families?" said Polk.

To that end, MGCCC aims to be a synergistic force for advancing economic prosperity across its region by anticipating and meeting the educational and training needs of its community. As the needs of students, employers, and the region's economy have shifted over time, so has the college's approach, which includes an intentional pivot away from the traditional approach to community college education. "There has been a devaluing of degrees and a replacement of that with folks that demonstrate they have skills and abilities," said Dr. Jonathan Woodward, executive vice president of teaching and learning/community campus. "One of the reasons there's this blurring of lines for us as an institution is that we're staying not just in lock step with where business and industry is but anticipating where it is going."

A Look at the Labor Market Landscape

According to Woodward, MGCCC is committed to staying ahead of shifting trends in the region by anticipating, developing, and delivering training that equips the region with the workforce it needs. In its strategic plan, Excelerate 2030, the college predicts that six sectors will exhibit strong job growth over the next ten years: the blue economy; healthcare; engineering technology; hospitality, tourism, and the creative economy; manufacturing and construction; and logistics and transportation.[13] Based on employment projections from the Mississippi Department of Employment Security, MGCCC's district is projected to experience 4.9 percent growth in employment from 2018 to 2028, with an average of 19,725 annual job openings.[14]

After an initial decline during the COVID-19 pandemic, Woodward said the region's hospitality and tourism industry is quickly recovering. In addition, the region produces several key naval vessels for the Navy and Coast Guard, and Woodward said local shipbuilding companies have contracts in place to continue building those ships over the next decade.

Some of the key industries in the college's four-county region include the following:

- *Shipbuilding:* Ingalls Shipbuilding, a division of Huntington-Ingalls Industries, is located in Pascagoula on eight hundred acres of land and employs 11,500 employees, making it the largest manufacturing employer in the state.[15] VT Halter Marine, another shipbuilding company, employs roughly one thousand people and focuses on construction of vessels for the military.
- *Energy and utilities:* Pascagoula Refinery is Chevron's largest US refinery. It employs 1,585 people and supports an additional 1,015 refinery jobs (contractors).[16] Mississippi Power serves 188,000 customers across twenty-three counties in Mississippi. Its large-scale solar facilities make it the state's largest partner in renewable energy.[17]
- *Aerospace:* Keesler Air Force Base is located in Harrison County and specializes in technical training of airmen following their basic training. On average, Keesler serves 2,700 students on the base at a time.[18]
- *Healthcare:* Singing River Health System has three hospitals and over nineteen clinics that employ roughly 3,600 people. Also nearby, Memorial Health System employs roughly 5,100 people.[19]
- *Hospitality and tourism:* Coastal Mississippi accounts for one-third of the state's tourism employees, expenditures, and taxes.[20] The region includes twelve casinos and numerous hotels and outdoor attractions.

The Student Makeup of MGCCC

As of the 2020–2021 school year, MGCCC served roughly one thousand more credit students (12,191),[21] which includes both academic and CTE enrollment, than it did noncredit trainees (11,107).[22] More than half of MGCCC's credit students are enrolled in academic programs, which are designed to meet the needs of students who seek to transfer to a four-year bachelor's degree.[23] Roughly a fourth of MGCCC's credit students are enrolled in CTE programs, which are designed to meet the needs of students who are seeking immediate employment or advancement within a career field.[24] The college's credit enrollment last peaked at 14,029 in the 2012–2013 school year and then declined through the 2019–2020 school year.[25]

Amid the COVID-19 pandemic, the college's credit enrollment experienced a slight increase in the 2020–2021 school year, growing to 12,191 from the 2019–2020 enrollment of 12,003.[26] According to Woodward, during this time, students gravitated toward sectors with higher salaries and more stability. For example, students shifted away from the hospitality sector, which was heavily disrupted by the pandemic, and toward the manufacturing and healthcare industries, which were more stable.

The number of unduplicated noncredit trainees the college served decreased slightly from 2020 to 2021, down to 11,107 from 12,469 in the 2019–2020 school year.[27] Woodward says participation was strongest in short-term, low-cost trainings that led to livable wages, such as noncredit welding courses.

Facing disruptions to traditional face-to-face learning, MGCCC also shifted instruction toward blended learning, which Woodward says uses a combination of face-to-face offerings, online options, and extended reality to deliver training. Using CARES Act funding, the college purchased technologies to enable the virtual delivery of instruction, including augmented reality and virtual reality (i.e., EON Reality solutions, smart boards, laptops, and simulators).[28]

Planning Ahead for the Next Decade

MGCCC's mission, vision, and values are codified in its new strategic plan—Excelerate 2030—which focuses on what type of institution the college wants to become in ten years. The four focus areas of the plan are teaching and learning, student experience, engagement and partnerships, and institutional excellence—all of which are informed by a desire for innovation and continuous improvement.[29] This plan is also the catalyst for many of the changes the college is now implementing, including both the schools model and the use of data to measure and rank all CTE programs.

At the conclusion of MGCCC's last strategic plan in 2020, the college worked to capture what its biggest accomplishments were over the previous ten years. According to Dr. Suzana Brown, executive vice president of institutional advancement for MGCCC, this included asking for faculty perspectives on what their biggest wins were and then pairing these anecdotes with data to back their claims up. After developing a presentation on those successes, Brown said the college met with as many community partners as it could, sharing where it had been and asking what the public wanted the college to become over the next ten years. The college also used survey technology called Poll Everywhere to collect feedback from both community leaders and internal employees, which informed the development of the new strategic plan.

Launched in fall 2020, Excelerate 2030 is divided into three-year sprint cycles that include assessment and adaptation at each step along the way. According to Woodward, the college is currently working to build a database that measures the success of the strategic plan in real time. At the end of the first three-year sprint in 2023, the college will stop, assess how its efforts are going so far, and determine if modifications are needed before entering the second three-year sprint. Even amid the uncertainty of the past few years during the COVID-19 pandemic, Woodward says that this long-term strategic plan reflects the fact that MGCCC "knows what we want to be when we grow up."

BREAKING DOWN SILOS: THE SCHOOLS MODEL AND STUDENT SUPPORTS

The Schools Model

In the fall of 2020, Mississippi Gulf Coast Community College overhauled its entire organizational structure. Unveiled as part of the college's ten-year strategic plan, the schools model intentionally blurs the lines among academic, CTE, and noncredit training. Its ultimate goal is to revolutionize the structure of the college in a way that emphasizes skills and workforce-aligned learning across all programs, credit and noncredit.

Two of the motivating factors behind this decision were to combat the entrenched stigmas associated with CTE and noncredit workforce training, as well as to eliminate the silos in knowledge between credit and noncredit students, faculty, and staff. For example, CTE would include courses taken in welding technology that earn credit toward an associate of applied science degree, while noncredit training would include a maritime pipe welding bootcamp.[30] "For a long time, there really has been a stigma against career and technical education programs," said Jonathan Woodward. "It was the programs in the back, dark part of campus. . . . It was not necessarily the place you wanted to send your children if you were a parent."

Suzana Brown began working with the college as an English professor twenty years ago. Back then, she said her knowledge of the college's noncredit workforce training efforts was narrow and limited. "I had always heard this term, *workforce*, but for many years . . . I didn't know what they did. I could tell you one company we worked with, and that was Ingalls Shipbuilding, but everyone could tell you that," said Brown. "I didn't really have intimate knowledge of the inner workings of [workforce training]."

For years, Mississippi Gulf Coast Community College has been working to change mindsets among its community, parents, and employers about what career and technical education and noncredit workforce training entail, aiming to increase knowledge about jobs with competitive wages that do not require a four-year bachelor's degree. According to Woodward, as part of those efforts, MGCCC began putting its money where its mouth was. The college invested in significant upgrades to career and technical education classrooms and workforce training equipment, transforming these spaces into bright, clean, and welcoming learning environments.

The next iteration of these efforts, which is to continue to knock down the walls between academic, CTE, and noncredit training, was the formal launch of the schools model.

BACKGROUND ON THE SCHOOLS MODEL

The schools model collapsed all of the college's former departments into one of eight topic-focused "schools" (plus the Honors College): business, law, hospitality, and culinary; engineering, mathematics, data science, and IT; manufacturing, maritime, and transportation; science and kinesiology; nursing and health professions; human sciences and education; language arts; and visual and performing arts.[31] These schools provide students with various options within similar areas of study to make their path to completion easier. For example, a student may choose a two-year technical path but then decide they want to continue their studies and transfer to a four-year institution, or a student may initially intend to transfer but then decide a CTE program is better for them. MGCCC's schools provide a clear road map for students to work toward certificates, diplomas, or degrees.

For example, take computer programming. According to Woodward, until recently, if an MGCCC student was enrolled in a two-year computer programming degree program on a four-year transfer pathway, they were in the academic Computer Programming department. But if a student was a computer programming major planning to complete the associate of applied science degree and then enter the workforce, they were in the Career and Technical Computer Programming department, even though they were studying the exact same thing. This meant siloed information and the duplication of resources, including different faculty chairs for academic computer programming versus career and technical computer programming.

The schools model is designed to blur these distinctions. Now, all students interested in computer science are within the School of Engineering, Mathematics, Data Science, and IT. That means CTE students are dispersed across the college's campus, rather than kept in one area as in the past. All faculty, whether academic, CTE, or noncredit, are placed on equal footing. "What's interesting is it's really had a huge impact on morale among our faculty. But more than that, on student morale," said Woodward. "CTE programs have come into the sunshine. They are no longer in the back of the campus where parents might be reluctant to send their children."

The collapse of multiple departments, each with its own faculty chair, into a single "school" also meant the reorganization of leadership positions across the college. For example, human physiology and recreation used to be its own department, but it now lives under the School of Sciences and Kinesiology. There used to be three chairs of human physiology and recreation and three chairs of science—one at each of the college's three campuses—for a total of six chairs. But under the new model, only three total chair positions remain. This meant redoing interviews and renaming chairs. "It allowed us to hit the reset button and change some things we knew needed to be changed about the chair structure, such as setting up a natural time frame that their chairmanship would be reviewed and offered an extension or not," said Woodward.

The model also created new positions—including an instructional designer and three advising coordinators for each school—to make student navigation easier and improve the collaborative spirit among academic, CTE, and noncredit faculty members.

THE ROLLOUT PROCESS

MGCCC's executive leadership knew this proposal would be perceived as revolutionary. The change comprised a radically different operating model for faculty and staff. To gain the community's buy-in before rolling the schools model out, leadership convened dinners at each of the college's three main campuses, where they shared their plans. "This was in January 2020. So, eight months before it happens, we're telling them, 'We know this is going to be volatile, but this is the way we need to go, and this is why we need to go there,'" said Woodward.

Dr. Jordan Sanderson, now the associate vice president of teaching and learning, was a faculty member and chair of the Language Arts department at the time that the schools model was announced.

"It brought the best to the top . . . and it created a more collaborative spirit. It introduced a real interdisciplinary mindset," said Sanderson. With the schools model, all faculty focused on a topic area are in the same meetings and the same places, allowing for the development of stronger courses with input from all.

According to Sanderson, another key result of the model has been a shift to a focus on skills that are in demand. Rather than thinking about traditional student learning outcomes, academic faculty members are now thinking about what students will be able to do with what they are learning. "The schools model facilitated a shift toward focusing on marketable skills, and that was definitely new for the academic side," said Sanderson.

The schools model has also allowed CTE students to feel more integrated and unified with the rest of the college and the opportunities it offers, from joining the Honors College to getting involved with Phi Theta Kappa, the honor society. "I think for the [CTE] students, it gave them this broad thing—I'm not choosing this or that, I'm still a part of the whole, I'm just specializing," said John Poelma, associate vice president of community campus and career technical education.

Dr. Erin Riggins, associate vice president of workforce solutions, said the rollout of the schools model came with both challenges and support. New school chairs, especially those who had only worked on the academic side, were often challenged and nervous—but the college's leadership provided them support throughout the transition. "It was definitely a culture change," said Riggins. "The good news is the one piece of the culture that was here from the beginning

> "The schools model facilitated a shift toward focusing on marketable skills, and that was definitely new for the academic side."
>
> *—Dr. Jordan Sanderson, Associate Vice President of Teaching and Learning, Mississippi Gulf Coast Community College*

and remained is we really have a faculty that is truly supportive of what is best for the student."

Supporting Student Navigation

ADVISING

In collaboration with the schools model, MGCCC also overhauled its advising system. When students apply to the college, they are immediately placed in a school-specific advising course on Canvas, the college's online learning management system. Once they register for classes, they are assigned to a full-time faculty member as their advisor within that Canvas course. "Imagine having a Canvas class that is solely for the purpose of your career and your learning community, and you're actually connected with other people and your faculty advisor before you ever step foot on campus," said Woodward.

The Canvas course includes general information about career trajectories, information on guided pathways, and details about student supports, including things like financial aid and the transferability of credits to four-year institutions. Woodward describes the student experience within these Canvas courses as a blend between a learning community and advising.

Another benefit of the schools model is that it allows advising to be more comprehensive. In the past, the college's advising was siloed; faculty members on the academic side likely couldn't speak to what a student's options would be on the CTE side and vice versa. Now, unified advising by subject area provides students with more information on all of their options for attaining a certificate, diploma, or degree. And while faculty members serving as advisors may not be commonplace across the community college realm, Graham says that it is a practice that is built into the college's culture. "We know the faculty are going to be more exposed to and more involved with their students than anyone else in the institution just by default," said Graham.

CAREER READINESS CENTERS

In conjunction with the college's existing career services, a new partnership with Goodwill Industries of South Mississippi will establish career readiness centers on MGCCC's campuses.[32] According to Tripp Harrison, president and CEO of Goodwill Industries of South Mississippi, Goodwill plays an important role in the region's workforce landscape by providing wraparound services to those facing barriers to employment. Now Goodwill will leverage those services for MGCCC, providing students with resume writing, interview skills, computer literacy skills, soft skill development, and more. "Our goal is to become a resource for MGCCC to help the students really prepare themselves to get out into the workforce on a journey to a successful career path, and we're going to be right there on their campus to help them get started on this journey," said Harrison. The first center is planned to open in fall 2022, with the ultimate goal being to have a center located at all three of the college's campuses.

STUDENT SUPPORT

One of the biggest things that stands out in Carlin Taylor's student experience at MGCCC has been the support he has received from faculty and staff. Taylor received his associate of arts degree from MGCCC in May 2021. He recently began another MGCCC program—an associate of applied science program in simulation and game design technology[33]—and intends to one day attend a four-year arts college.

According to Taylor, MGCCC has been a game changer for his future. He says the college has helped him fine-tune exactly what he wants to do in the future—3D character animation—and what future career paths are available to him. Faculty and staff at the college, from his honors advisor to various campus deans to President Graham, have all provided Taylor with direct support throughout his time as a student. "Faculty here at Gulf Coast are absolutely amazing. They kept every relationship we had personal; it felt like they genuinely cared about my progress, my future, my development," said Taylor.

In 2022, Taylor was named a Jack Kent Cooke Undergraduate Transfer Scholar by Phi Theta Kappa, a distinction that Taylor credits in part to the support he received from MGCCC faculty and staff. Taylor's experience reflects the strong emphasis that MGCCC places on supporting its students. In addition to traditional supports such as food pantries and clothing closets, Woodward says MGCCC also works to anticipate challenges students may face before they occur. One way the college does this is through a financial aid alert system. The college developed a novel technology that uses predictive analytics to warn students who are at risk of not meeting satisfactory academic progress (SAP) requirements, which would cause them to lose access to federal student aid.[34] For example, the college can use the system to alert students about the number of credits they need to take or the grade they need to achieve to ensure they continue meeting SAP requirements. "It's not just being reactive in wraparound services—it's being proactive," said Woodward.

Graham said MGCCC also invests in its students through scholarships, including a dedicated $5.9 million in the college's operations budget for student scholarships, in addition to what the college's foundation provides.

Another system the college uses is called Early Alert. It tracks metrics such as attendance to understand how students are doing. It also has an area where administrators, staff, and faculty can enter notes about individual students' needs, which are then forwarded to enrollment services and appropriate college personnel. "If we notice the student has transportation issues, we have funds and we can get them a bus pass. We bought someone a bicycle one time," said Woodward. Other examples of resources students can be connected to include childcare centers reserved solely for MGCCC students with children and free health clinics.

INVESTING IN RELATIONSHIPS: EMPLOYERS AND THE COMMUNITY

Strengthening Employer Relationships

MGCCC prioritizes building and maintaining deep relationships with local businesses and industries by doing everything in its power to best meet workforce development needs. "They know that if they need something and they call us, we're going to do everything within our power to make it happen, and that it's going to be good," said Dr. Erin Riggins, MGCCC's associate vice president of workforce solutions.

Michael Leleux, recruiting and training manager with VT Halter Marine, says his job would be more difficult without MGCCC. The college offers numerous workforce solutions to VT Halter Marine, including apprenticeship programs and a variety of noncredit workforce training classes on things like technology solutions and AutoCAD. According to Leleux, the response to every request he has made to the college over the years has exceeded his ex-

pectations. "Without the college, I think we'd
be a sinking ship," said Leleux. "The partnership that we have established with the college
through the years is to me immeasurable because of the relationships I have over there. . . .
I dream it, they make it happen."

Three factors contribute to MGCCC's
strong employer relationships: integrating
credit and noncredit offerings, an iterative pro-

> "Without the college, I think we'd
> be a sinking ship. The partner-
> ship that we have established
> with the college through the
> years is to me immeasurable
> because of the relationships I
> have over there. . . . I dream it,
> they make it happen."
>
> *—Michael Leleux,*
> *Recruiting and*
> *Training Manager,*
> *VT Halter Marine*

cess focused on meeting employers' needs, and a culture of flexibility and
innovation.

INTEGRATING CREDIT AND NONCREDIT OFFERINGS

Recognizing that employers' needs may be best served by noncredit or credit
offerings, Dr. Riggins and Poelma work hand in hand to support employers' requests. Often in the first meetings with an employer, both Riggins and
Poelma show up to the table together to understand how to best meet the
employer's needs, allowing them to answer questions and provide information on options up front. Riggins's and Poelma's offices at the college are even
located side by side.

For example, according to Riggins, an employer may contact a CTE in-
structor with a request for a credit offering, or they may reach out to the workforce solutions team with a request for noncredit training. Regardless, Riggins
and Poelma work together to determine what will best meet the employer's
needs—credit or noncredit—and identify what supports are available for that
programming, from equipment to funding. Riggins said the college recently
leveraged equipment from a CTE program for a noncredit training need as
part of an advanced technology and advanced manufacturing program.

This close partnership between noncredit and credit programs allows the
college to be nimble and responsive to workforce development needs, says
Riggins. "Industry moves at the speed of light, so we have to be able to work
at that speed, and often times education doesn't move that fast," she said. "We
can use each other's expertise, the support of the faculty, and the equipment
to make something happen really fast."

ITERATIVE PROCESS FOCUSED ON MEETING EMPLOYERS'
NEEDS

When employers approach the college, they are often uncertain about what they need, says Riggins. They have likely identified a pain point—such as the need to increase productivity or to train employees on a new process. They might need equipment, instructors, and funding support. According to Riggins, rather than providing quick one-off responses to initial employer requests, MGCCC aims to work in tandem with the employer to peel back the layers and understand what they truly need.

This includes walking the employer through their training options, how the training will work, and how long it will take. MGCCC staff engage in active listening and frequent communication with employers throughout an iterative process that aims to understand their needs. Sometimes, this means that an initial employer meeting will not result in a project right away, but these conversations open the door for the employer to come back to the college in the future. According to Poelma, this shows employers that the college is not interested in simply selling a product; instead, it is offering honest advice, and that strengthens the college's relationship with employers.

In addition, once a workforce need has been identified, MGCCC does whatever it takes to meet that need. For example, take Mississippi Power, a utilities company that serves roughly 188,000 customers across twenty-three counties in Mississippi. As a long-standing partner of MGCCC, Mississippi Power has worked with the college to open an instrumentation and control technology center and a forthcoming lineman school in Harrison County.

According to Tommy Murphy, vice president of customer service and operations at Mississippi Power, all of his conversations with MGCCC have focused on how to get to "yes." During their initial meeting with MGCCC, Murphy said Dr. Graham was in attendance, along with numerous other members of the college's leadership. Murphy said that this visible show of commitment from the college's president set the tone for the rest of the partnership.

For Ann Holland, workforce development and education coordinator with Mississippi Power, the college's secret sauce is its people. "From the top to the bottom, they're all just willing and focused on 'How can we make it happen?' I don't know that I've ever been told 'No, we can't do that,'" said Holland.

Apprenticeship Models at MGCCC

One of the cornerstones of MGCCC's workforce development offerings are apprenticeships, earn while you learn programs in which registered apprentices gain on-the-job work experience alongside related classroom instruction, resulting in a nationally recognized credential within the industry upon completion.

After studying Germany's vocational education training system, MGCCC alumnus Deeneaus Polk was recruited as the director of the Mississippi Apprenticeship Program (MAP). When Polk began in this role, he said the concept of apprenticeships was not widespread in Mississippi. According to Polk, for some community colleges in the state at that time, it was a hard sell due to the way that apprenticeships had become politicized. However, Polk says this wasn't the case at MGCCC, which had long been a leader in this space due to its decades-old apprenticeship program with Ingalls Shipbuilding. "In regard to workforce, the college has always been a progressive institution that is really focused on 'How do we create the programmatic structures that are impacting people in a positive way and actually getting people good jobs?'" said Polk.

Although apprenticeships at MGCCC date back to the 1950s, the college is reimagining their potential for workforce advancement in new ways, creating unique apprenticeship models in nontraditional sectors, including finance and healthcare. Three examples highlight the college's work on apprenticeships: launching apprenticeships with MAP, the college's long-standing partnership with Ingalls Shipbuilding, and a new apprenticeship program with Singing River Health System.

LAUNCHING APPRENTICESHIPS WITH THE MISSISSIPPI APPRENTICESHIP PROGRAM

MAP assists companies in developing registered apprenticeships, from the initial concept through implementation. The program is funded by Department of Labor grants[35] and is housed within the Mississippi Department of Employment Security. MAP partners with several community colleges across the state to support their workforce efforts by providing registered apprenticeship grant funds. At MGCCC, Gayle Brown, workforce and special projects developer, works hand in hand with Tonya Neely, director of MAP, to assist local employers in developing apprenticeships.

According to Brown, MGCCC supports apprenticeship programs across six different employers, with programs ranging in size from small cohorts at Rolls Royce to cohorts of seventy-plus apprentices at Ingalls Shipbuilding. Each apprenticeship program has two components—related training instruction, in which students learn content in class; and on-the-job training, in which students apply what they have learned.

Each time a new registered apprenticeship program is created, Brown says a curriculum has to be written that maps what content will be learned during lectures with what skills will be covered during on-the-job training and details how much time will be spent on each of those skills. According to Brown, this is often the most daunting part of the process: the curriculum writer has to identify resources, from books to PowerPoint presentations, and merge those with what the apprentice is expected to learn on the job. Funding from MAP supports the hiring of curriculum developers that work in partnership with MGCCC to accomplish this.

According to Brown and Neely, the benefits of apprenticeship programs for both apprentices and employers are multifold.

Brown has seen firsthand the difference apprenticeship programs have made in the lives of graduates, allowing them to advance to the middle class and achieve goals such as securing a loan for a home. For Dr. Riggins, the college's associate vice president of workforce solutions, apprenticeship programs are also a crucial way that the college can achieve its mission of helping industry partners meet their workforce goals. "If they're able to increase production, retain employees, and many times get new apprentices to join the program . . . then that's success for us," said Riggins.

A LONG-STANDING PARTNERSHIP: INGALLS APPRENTICE SCHOOL

Since 1952, Ingalls Shipbuilding, a division of Huntington-Ingalls Industries, has partnered with MGCCC on apprenticeship programs.[38] Ingalls is the sponsor of the program that coordinates on-the-job training and Department of Labor requirements, while MGCCC provides classroom instruction.[39] Currently, the Ingalls Apprentice School offers fifteen registered apprenticeship programs that serve 280 active apprentices—including electricians, pipe welders, and carpenters—and range in length from two to four years.[40]

Benefits of Apprenticeship

- *Completing credits debt-free:* Registered apprentices participate in the program for free, providing access to courses and training they might have otherwise had to pay for. They are also paid for the job they are working as they develop new skills.
- *Access to resources:* Brown says one thing she hears often from apprentices is that the best part of the program is the access to information and people within the company that they would not otherwise have.
- *National certification:* Apprentices that complete the program receive a nationally recognized Certificate of Completion of Apprenticeship from the Department of Labor, providing the flexibility to take that certification elsewhere in the industry.[36]
- *Career advancement:* While some apprenticeship programs recruit apprentices externally, others open their programs only to existing employees, providing a pathway for career advancement to those who otherwise may not be able to advance into a higher role without going back to school.
- *Recruitment advantages:* Singing River Health System, one of the college's apprenticeship partners, includes its apprenticeship programs as part of its benefit package and promotes them on social media as a recruiting tool.
- *Increased retention:* According to the Department of Labor, 92 percent of apprentices who complete an apprenticeship program retain employment, with an average annual salary of $72,000.[37]

Damita Caldwell is a second-generation shipbuilder who has worked with Ingalls Shipbuilding for twenty-four years. Now, as the director of operations for workforce training and development, Caldwell is responsible for new hire training, incumbent training of existing employees, and the apprenticeship program. According to Caldwell, MGCCC offers strong support when it comes to educational resources, including access to important software like Canvas. Amid the COVID-19 pandemic, Ingalls worked to shift some of its apprenticeship components online, and Caldwell says MGCCC played a key role in equipping Ingalls to provide coursework remotely.

Over the course of the last few decades, Caldwell says that Ingalls apprenticeships have changed. In the past, the only way to get hired as a craftsperson with no prior experience was through an apprenticeship program. Now, incumbent employees have an opportunity to become apprentices. For example, if an employee is originally hired as a paint helper but wants to go into a different craft, such as electrical, they can apply and have first priority for apprenticeship positions. In addition, the apprentice program used to be held during the evening hours after traditional work shifts. Now, Caldwell says students attend class during their regular shift on the clock—allowing them to be paid to attend apprenticeship classes.

To better meet the training needs of Ingalls apprentices, MGCCC decided to physically come to them. In 2013, the college opened the Haley Reeves Barbour Maritime Training Academy, located just outside the main gate of Ingalls Shipbuilding in Pascagoula.[41]

A NEW APPRENTICESHIP WITH LICENSED PRACTICAL NURSES AT SINGING RIVER HEALTH SYSTEM

Singing River Health System employs over 3,600 people across three hospitals and nineteen supporting clinics along the Mississippi Gulf Coast. Jessica Lewis became the system's executive human resources director just before the COVID-19 pandemic hit, and since then, the labor market for healthcare employees has changed drastically. According to Lewis, the system's employee turnover rate before the pandemic was roughly 16 to 18 percent, but now the system is facing an unprecedented turnover rate of 36 percent or more. Nursing shortages that existed before COVID-19 have been further exacerbated. Over the last year, Lewis says the system hired almost two thousand people— four to five times what it was hiring before the pandemic.

To address these workforce challenges, one of Lewis's first priorities was to build up the hospital system's internal employee development pipeline by creating registered apprenticeship programs. Through conversations with Gayle Brown, workforce and special projects director at MGCCC, Lewis discussed what the system's pain points and difficulties were. From there, Singing River

Health System developed numerous apprenticeships for technical programs, including certified nursing assistants and phlebotomy.

Recently, Singing River Health System launched a new pilot program in partnership with MGCCC: the first LPN apprenticeship in the state of Mississippi, according to Lewis. According to Brown, the college called every other state with an LPN apprenticeship program—of which MGCCC identified only four in the country—and learned that all of those programs were credit models, which meant employers had to pay tuition for their apprentices to take for-credit courses at the community college. According to Brown, MGCCC pitched this idea to Singing River Health System as an alternative to address the need to hire nurses quickly: it would pilot the first noncredit LPN apprenticeship program, creating what it believes is the first of its kind in the nation.

Apprentices in the program are paid to attend classes two days a week and then paid for the remaining two or three days that they spend gaining clinical work experience, says Lewis. At the end of the fourteen-month program, they will gain an LPN license. If graduated apprentices then decide they want to become registered nurses (RNs), they can continue through MGCCC's hybrid LPN to RN program.[42] "It really opens it up to so many people that have always wanted to go back to school but can't," said Lewis. "Hospital schedules and education schedules don't always match up, so it's sitting at the table and developing it so that it works together."

According to Lewis, MGCCC was instrumental in bringing this pilot program to fruition, including listening to the system's needs and coming up with a solution. The college also assisted in talking to the state's nursing board and getting the program passed through necessary regulatory processes.

After posting the LPN apprenticeship application internally for three days, Lewis says more than 120 Singing River Health System employees applied for just twenty seats. The first pilot program began on April 11, 2022. Lewis says this program is the hospital system's lifeline for being able to fill critical positions in the future and that it provides advantages that set Singing River Health System apart from its competitors. "We want people to know that once they come in here, they can continually grow and develop. And that's what's going to retain and help fill all these great needs, because there's so many positions that need to be filled, and this is going to be the key," said Lewis.

To determine the success of the program, Lewis said Singing River Health System will track retention rates and whether or not graduates continue on to additional training programs. In the future, Singing River Health System hopes to grow the program to about two hundred LPN apprentices per year.

OFFERING PROFESSIONAL DEVELOPMENT THROUGH APPRENTICESHIPS WITH KEESLER FEDERAL CREDIT UNION

A flexible and innovative approach to workforce solutions allows MGCCC to stretch beyond the status quo when it comes to designing workforce trainings. Even when an employer's request is unprecedented, MGCCC does everything within its power to offer a solution.

After many years of working with the college on various workforce development needs, Ruth Montana, director of human resources for Keesler Federal Credit Union, approached the college with a desire to offer employees an opportunity for professional development. Through a partnership with the college over the course of a year, Montana said that she learned about all the types of apprenticeship models that were available to Keesler and ultimately landed on a two-and-a-half-year apprenticeship program for employees to train to become branch managers. According to Montana, this was the first time that a Mississippi employer offered an apprenticeship program within the financial industry.

Keesler then pitched the apprenticeship program to employees across its forty branches. According to Montana, they heard from employees who were interested in the program but would not be able to physically take classes at an MGCCC campus because they worked in branches in other states, including Alabama and Louisiana. With that feedback, Montana said they realized Keesler would need to offer this program online, but at the time, MGCCC did not offer any noncredit workforce training programs online. "And they said 'Well, if that's what you need, we're going to make it happen," said Montana.

MGCCC did make it happen, and Keesler Federal Credit Union became the first employer in the state to offer a noncredit workforce training online. Initially, the program planned to admit only ten applicants—but twenty-eight employees applied, so the company decided to give them all apprenticeships, said Montana.

So far, the program has proven to be successful. According to Montana, 89 percent of employees in the program that apply for promotions to branch manager positions are successfully promoted. Investing in their employees in this way has allowed Keesler to build loyalty and commitment within its employees, says Montana.

Staying Engaged with the Community

Beyond employer relationships, the college also invests in deep connections within its four-county service area through a variety of community engagement efforts.

ADVISORY COUNCILS

All fifty-six CTE programs have an advisory council with industry representatives who hire and train for their respective companies. The councils meet with CTE instructors twice a year or more, helping the college keep a pulse on industry trends and ensuring that CTE programming stays relevant and aligned with what is happening in the field. According to Dr. Suzana Brown, executive vice president of institutional advancement, this structure has caused a shift from what could be a competitive relationship with employers—such as employers wanting to hire students before they have completed programs—to a collaborative relationship focused on how to build the strongest partnerships through opportunities like internships and apprenticeships.

The advisory councils also provide feedback about the strengths and weaknesses of the students they have hired, allowing the college to modify its CTE programming accordingly. For example, after hearing employer feedback that students were falling behind in certain soft skills, such as punctuality and communication, Brown said MGCCC created a Quality Enhancement Plan called Embracing Essential Skills that focuses on attendance and punctuality, listening, and speaking.[43]

BEING AT THE TABLE

Every executive council staff member at the college serves on local boards, including chambers of commerce and Rotary clubs. Brown says this involvement has been crucial to strengthening the college's community relationships.

The college aims to be at the table when the workforce is being discussed in any capacity. This provides an opportunity to educate community members about the types of offerings the college has and how they have evolved over the years. "We're not the community college that we were in 1989," said Brown. "Students can come in and do these high-tech, high-demand, high-wage programs in two years and be extremely successful. And so being immersed in the community is what that's all about."

Accelerate MS: Working with the State to Acquire Funding

While some states have long had workforce development offices that assess labor needs and guide people toward in-demand skills, Mississippi historically did not. There was no single repository for workforce development information and no structure to determine if those investments were actually leading people to better jobs.[44] Many stakeholders, including President Graham, recognized the need for better collaboration and coordination of resources for workforce development efforts.

Then, in 2020, a report found that the State of Mississippi spends roughly $350 million in state and federal funds on workforce development and training each year.[45] Facing one of the lowest labor force participation rates in the country,[46] some legislators felt that the state was not collecting the right information to understand the impact of those dollars or how they were being used.[47] "How are we training? Are we doing it in schools? How is that going? Are the community colleges meeting the needs? Where are they not meeting the needs? Is everything running as smoothly as it should?" Lt. Gov. Delbert Hosemann told *Mississippi Today.*[48]

Hoping to make advancements in workforce training efforts, Mississippi legislators decided to restructure the way workforce development efforts are funded. In 2020, Mississippi Governor Tate Reeves signed legislation that created the Mississippi Office of Workforce Development, known as Accelerate Mississippi (Accelerate MS), within the state's Department of Finance and Administration. Now, Mississippi's fifteen community colleges have a single point of contact that is tasked with thinking about how to continuously improve the state's workforce development efforts, from assisting companies interested in moving into the state to supporting the needs of existing industries.

Under the direction of Executive Director Ryan Miller, Accelerate MS strives to operate as the "tip of the spear" for the state's workforce strategy development and deployment. The office's goal is to align resources to meet workforce needs more effectively and efficiently, thus leading more Mississippians to skills training and well-paying jobs.[49] "We're supposed to be the teammate here in the state capitol to help develop . . . strategy, and then find the resources at a statewide level that we can utilize, procure, and deploy to help support those strategies with our partners, like Mississippi Gulf Coast Community College," said Miller.

Prior to the creation of Accelerate MS, Miller said that redundancy and duplication of efforts were common, minimizing the effectiveness of workforce development investments. In an effort to better maximize the benefits of workforce development funds, Accelerate MS has adopted an ecosystem approach that works to "set the table" in each of the state's regions by convening stakeholders across eight sectors.[50] Representatives from each of these sectors discuss their unique workforce training needs to inform Accelerate MS's funding strategy.

Accelerate MS has oversight of two different funding sources from the state: the Workforce Enhancement Training (WET) fund and the Mississippi Works fund.

Funded through the state's unemployment trust fund that employers pay into via taxes, WET funds are awarded to community colleges to administer based on training needs and requests from employers. WET funds were previously under the domain of the state's Community College Board and are now dispersed from Accelerate MS, although the board is still involved in processing the funds.

Mississippi Works was established in 2016 when the legislature allocated $50 million over ten years to help community colleges and other workforce training programs increase their operations. It was previously administered by the Mississippi Development Authority, the economic development state agency, but is now administered by Accelerate MS. As of March 2020, less than 10 percent of the funding had been spent.[51]

In April 2022, Gov. Reeves provided an update on the state's workforce development efforts, including the progress of Accelerate MS, and signed legislation that provides additional funding for workforce development efforts and greater flexibility for the use of Mississippi Works funds.[52] "We've continued building a pipeline that will streamline the training of a next-generation workforce," said Gov. Reeves.

According to Woodward, Accelerate Mississippi has streamlined workforce training for the entire state in terms of both focus and resources. "The formation of Accelerate MS established a more sustainable workforce training model via the braiding of funds to minimize costs and maximize impact," said Woodward.

Miller's hope is that the existence of ecosystem relationships allows Accelerate MS to be in close contact with partners about what their needs are, and then to respond efficiently and accurately with the right resources to meet those needs. To that end, he says one of MGCCC's strengths is operating in a collaborative and responsive way to meet the needs of the college's community. "I know they've done a great job of being able to serve because they know who they're serving," said Miller.

A CULTURE OF CONTINUOUS IMPROVEMENT: DATA-DRIVEN DECISION-MAKING

Understanding the Health of CTE Programs

How should a community college with dozens of CTE programs understand and compare program outcomes to make informed decisions about its future? At MGCCC, a robust set of metrics are aggregated into a single health score for all fifty-six CTE programs, allowing the college's administration to quickly understand how its performance compares and where opportunities and challenges exist. Launched as part of the college's ten-year strategic plan, there is now a parallel effort underway to develop a similar set of health metrics for the college's academic programs.

"We want to be relevant, but we're willing to shut down programs. If we don't see the job placement numbers that we should be seeing, if we don't see the enrollment or retention we should be seeing, we will shut down programs," said Jonathan Woodward. "Conversely, we've added a lot of programs."

The use of health metrics contributes to the college's desire to build a culture of continuous improvement that strives toward optimization, ensuring that the programs the college is offering are best meeting the needs of all stakeholders, from students to employers.

BUILDING A DATA WAREHOUSE

Dr. Adam Swanson, executive vice president of institutional effectiveness and research, is always thinking about what optimization looks like for his office—and he says that is a question that took him a long time to answer. Swanson manages planning for the college's roughly one hundred departments, all federal and state reporting requirements, internal reporting, survey research, accreditation, and more. When Swanson first began in the role, he said data requests were coming in every day with different specifics for how data should be disaggregated —from race to age to gender.

Then it clicked: the college needed a data warehouse that could function like a calculator, quickly generating the answer to any question across a variety of variables, says Swanson.

When Swanson first brought on a new team of programmers and data scientists, he gave them a simple yet challenging goal: to be able to answer any question in higher education in two minutes or less. In the five years since, Swanson's small team has built a data warehouse that now consists of more than three billion cells.

Swanson says the warehouse is the engine of the vehicle that powers all of the college's research, data, and planning capabilities, fueling dozens of interactive Tableau dashboards that track more than 130 variables and disaggregate them by various subgroups, including race, age, and gender. The tables are updated daily at midnight, ensuring that the warehouse reflects real-time information.

Just as a vehicle is only as powerful as its engine, Swanson says the college's reporting capabilities are only as strong as the data warehouse. This means that Swanson's team members have spent most of their time and energy ensuring that they built the data warehouse in an optimized way, drawing on research into best practices in academics and business, from the Ivy League to IBM.

According to Swanson, the power of the data warehouse's design is not in the individual tables it generates, but what happens when you join the tables together. "For example, your student enrollment table has seven hundred unique attributes for a particular student, but then you can connect that to the financial aid table, you can connect that to the schedule table," said Swanson. "When you connect that, you can answer any question pretty efficiently."

CREATING A SYSTEM OF HEALTH METRICS

Equipped with the engine of the data warehouse, MGCCC established a set of health metrics by which to understand the performance of all fifty-six CTE programs.

In Swanson's first year at the college, he said different CTE programs were measuring the same outcome in different ways, making it difficult or impossible to compare their results. For example, one CTE program might track retention from one fall semester to the next fall semester, while another might track it over a three-year period. Swanson described this time as a period of chaos; he quickly recognized the need for a set of shared metrics that were measured uniformly across the college. "The problem with our process was we had tons of documentation, and that's great, up until the point of [knowing] which program is actually knocking it out of the park and which is underperforming," said Swanson.

Then a moment of inspiration hit. While playing fantasy football, Swanson noticed that the system quantifies and ranks every NFL football player out of a set number of points, which made it easier for him to pick a strong team. He also thought back to his time working in industry, when he used a system that assigned job candidates a total score out of a set number of points based on how they scored on a number of variables in a matrix.

With that, the idea for the college's CTE health metrics was born. Swanson set out to create a system of standardized metrics that produce a quantitative score up to one thousand points, allowing the college to quickly understand which programs are and are not performing optimally.

Swanson says the first step was creating a set of standardized metrics, assigning them appropriate weights, and ensuring that they did not disadvantage certain kinds of programs. To do this, the college engaged a variety of stakeholders to decide what would make a CTE program "healthy," including faculty, industry partners, and program chairs. "The metrics have got to be rock solid, and there needs to be justification," said Swanson. "You have one thousand points, and so you have to weight these accordingly. If you give one metric five hundred points and all the other metrics very few points, that creates a lot of pressure on certain metrics." The nuance of each metric reflects the intentionality behind them. For example, Metric 1, distinct headcount by declared major; Metric 2, total FTE by subject; and Metric 3, course capacity; all contribute to a holistic understanding of the college's enrollment. See the Health Metrics box for a full list of the metrics.

"Let's say you're a business major: we have two hundred business majors, great. A different measurement is: how many people are taking business classes?" said Woodward. "Without having a full understanding of both, I don't have a full picture of enrollment."

Course capacity is a percent of total capacity to ensure that programs with stricter size limits—like culinary or chemistry—are not penalized for their smaller size. Metric 4, student pass rate by subject, is assigned 0 points in the system to avoid incentives for artificially passing students. Metric 6 was selected intentionally as fall to spring retention rather than fall to fall retention because many of the CTE programs are one year in duration.

In addition, most of these metrics are assigned point values based on the percentage of the metric value rather than the raw value in order to ensure the system doesn't unfairly advantage larger programs. Because the data is kept in Tableau and updated each night, the health metrics always use the most up-to-date data to determine how CTE programs are doing.

As with many of MGCCC's processes, the metrics themselves are designed to be iterative. The college's ten-year strategic plan includes multiple cycles, and at the end of each three-year sprint, Woodward said the college will reevaluate the metrics system and ask if these are still the right metrics to be using.

MGCCC has received national recognition for its health metrics system, presenting at conferences and in webinars to explain its process. Swanson said the college has had preliminary conversations about patenting its data warehouse structure and design, especially the college's automated reporting system that feeds into reports for the national Integrated Postsecondary Education Data System (IPEDS).

The college also has Tableau dashboards of data on noncredit enrollment, including head count information and analysis by subject area, educational attainment, and other demographics.

Health Metrics

There are thirteen metrics currently used by the system:

1. *Distinct headcount by declared major*: 25 points. The goal is to increase enrollment from year to year.
2. *Total FTE by subject*: 100 points. The goal is to increase full-time equivalency (FTE) from year to year.
3. *Course capacity*: 175 points. The goal is to have 100 percent capacity.
4. *Student pass rate by subject*: 0 points. This metric was included in the system for tracking purposes but given a zero-point value to avoid creating perverse incentives to inflate student grades and pass rates.
5. *FTE per faculty member*: 200 points. The goal is for each full-time faculty member to maintain 26 FTEs.
6. *Fall to spring retention*: 125 points. The goal is for each program to have a 75 percent fall to spring retention rate.
7. *Completion rate*: 100 points. The goal is for each program to have a 60 percent completion rate, as defined by completion of a thirty-hour credential, forty-five-hour credential, or degree.
8. *Distinct number of graduates by academic year*: 50 points. The goal is to increase the number of distinct graduates in a program.
9. *Technical skill attainment*: 25 points. The goal is for each program to maintain a 90 percent pass rate on the Perkins technical skill assessment.[53]
10. *Student placement of leavers*: 175 points. The goal is for each program to place 90 percent of leavers in a job.
11. *Student feedback on the annual student satisfaction survey*: 25 points. The goal is for each program to have 100 percent of the responses to the twelve instructional questions rated higher than the national average.[54]
12. *Graduate feedback on the graduate exit survey*: 0 points.
13. *Employer feedback on the employer satisfaction survey*: 0 points.

PERFORMANCE EVALUATION

According to Woodward, the system was given the name *health metrics* to reflect the fact that the college uses these data points as a way to understand how well each CTE program is doing, just as a doctor would use medical diagnoses to understand how healthy their patient is. "Some of these metrics are aneurism or coronary heart failure metrics; if those are an issue, the survival and sustainability of your program is in question," Woodward said.

According to Swanson, based on the standard deviation of the mean score, an annual point summary places CTE programs in one of three categories: green, yellow, or red. Programs with scores higher than one standard deviation above the mean are in green, indicating that they are performing most strongly. Programs within one standard deviation above the mean are in yellow, and programs below the mean are in red. "Green means you're good. Red means you have a coronary heart failure: we are firing up the defibrillator," said Woodward. "And at a threshold point in the yellow, we begin looking."

The annual point summary, described in the Health Metrics box, is the college's starting point for identifying which CTE programs are and are not performing optimally. From there, individual reports for each metric can provide further detail behind the aggregate health metric score. One report provides the rank of every CTE program from top to bottom for that metric, and a second report provides the historical data for that metric. These metric-specific reports also provide a variety of filters. For example, you can break the metric out for each program by variables like gender, disability, and race.

There are also specific reports that aggregate all of a program's metrics in one place, providing quick answers to common questions program directors may have, such as the number of applications, the number of enrolled credit hours, the amount of financial aid, and more.

At the end of each school year, Woodward says the president receives a binder with all of the health metric results for each CTE program, as well as an annual point summary that ranks them by total. In the meantime, a copy is also sent to each campus's vice president for their review. After the data has been reviewed, a meeting to discuss the results is convened with the college's director of institutional research, the leader of career and technical education, the leader of workforce training, the executive vice president of teaching and learning, and the president, with the campus vice presidents also invited to

attend. Then, the president determines the point threshold below which programs will be required to create an improvement plan.

PLANNING AND IMPROVEMENT

The specificity of the health metric system means that programs are not asked
for general improvement plans; instead, they drill down into specific areas
with the biggest need for growth. "We identify what the specific health metrics are that the program has a problem with, and within the health metric,
what particular groups they're not having success with," said Woodward. "We
really can get down to the microbial level of helping faculty and program leaders understand, 'Here's specifically where I have a problem and the things that
I need to do to impact change.'"

The college's planning system is also linked to the Tableau reports generated by the college's data warehouse. Rather than tasking every department
head with collecting and reporting their metrics, Swanson says his department
autopopulates the vast majority of every planning report using automated
fields that pull data from the tables in the data warehouse. This provides a
similar structure across all planning documents, with the time period, metric
definitions, expected outcomes, and results all prefilled by the college's Office
of Institutional Research and Effectiveness. "The reason we do this is we don't
want our auto mechanics and culinary arts folks putting in their mental energy trying to find the information. We want them spending time on the use
of results," said Swanson.

When Swanson first unveiled this new autopopulated planning system,
he said faculty members were thrilled. But Swanson told them it came with
a trade-off: in return, he asks that they focus on how to improve in metrics
where they are falling behind. Ultimately, Swanson wants this process to op-
timize all of the college's CTE programs, with each receiving a health metric
score higher than nine hundred points. "If you're overseeing a program and
your retention rate is 50 percent, for example, that means 50 percent of your
students did not return. That's a problem. So, what we're asking in your time,
expertise, all your mental energy is: How do you retain students at a higher
rate?" said Swanson. "You have to come up with some intervention, you have
to test that intervention."

The college's planning process also ensures that program departments are explicit about the actions they are taking to drive improvement within each metric. The right-most column of each planning document provides space for instructors to comment on how they are using the results and what their plan for improvement is, providing granular context behind each data point.

Reflecting on his first year at the college, Swanson remembers that data was often characterized by high-stress situations where faculty were up against deadlines, trying to pull together the information they needed. Now, faculty and staff have automated access to the streamlined data they need, allowing their focus to be on improving their programs rather than finding data. To encourage buy-in to the system, Swanson said it was important to use proactive communications with faculty and staff about why the college is using data the way it is.

Advancing Equity Initiatives by Using Data

In July 2020, as a result of the college's new strategic plan, the MGCCC Board of Trustees renamed the Jefferson Davis Campus to the Harrison County Campus.[55] Dr. Graham was also part of a nine-member commission[56] that designed a new Mississippi flag that was ratified in 2021,[57] replacing the previous flag that included a Confederate symbol. "The whole community here is eyes wide open to the legacy of Mississippi, and the place from which we've come, and the place where we want to be," said Dr. Woodward.

As the college strives for a more equitable future, it works to close equity gaps at each step of a student's journey, from access to enrollment to completion to placement. The robust nature of the college's database allows for outcomes to be disaggregated and subdivided across dozens of groups, including age, gender, race/ethnicity, and socioeconomic status based on financial aid data.

Access involves working to ensure the student body is at least as diverse as the local community the college serves. According to Woodward, the college currently enrolls a higher percentage of students of color than the percentage of those populations in the four-county region. For enrollment, the college aims to close equity gaps in programs with high livable wages, such as engineering, by encouraging students who are underrepresented in those programs to consider them. Woodward says the college also hosts nontraditional sum-mits, which are targeted recruitment events for fields that lack diversity, such as women in welding.

Closing equity gaps in completion often relates to disaggregating comple-tion data by subgroup. "We can look at a program and say, 'Listen, the people with the lowest socioeconomic status, they're not completing your program,'" said Woodward. "That's the challenge. So, what do we need to do? We need to go find scholarships; we need to do something for that population for barrier mitigation."

Finally, placement looks at equity gaps in both transfer rates to four-year universities and job placement rates.

Beyond student success, President Graham says the college is focused on diversity, equity, and inclusion in its own hiring practices. "I think it's impor-tant that students are comfortable in the classroom, in the labs—that they see people who look like them," said Graham. "Our goal is to make sure that everyone has an opportunity to be educated in a field that they can thrive in and earn a livable wage."

CONCLUSION

Mississippi Gulf Coast Community College recognizes that in order to cata-lyze economic growth in its region, it must constantly evolve to meet the needs of students and employers. To do so, the college has reimagined educa-tion in a way that intentionally blurs the traditional lines between credit and noncredit training and focuses more on skills than degrees. But these efforts are not static; instead, a culture of continuous improvement encourages staff and faculty to constantly adapt as new data is discovered and new trends emerge. Each of the main pillars of MGCCC's workforce strategy—includ-ing the schools model, investments in strong employer relationships, and the use of data to inform decision-making—is itself an iterative process that the college will return to numerous times over the course of its ten-year strategic plan, Excelerate 2030.

As MGCCC works to build the workforce of the future, its efforts cannot be fully understood without considering the communities it serves. The col-lege's location in a state with high poverty rates, low educational attainment rates, and historic inequities makes it even more imperative to build strong talent pipelines that meet the workforce needs of employers and offer sustainable employment opportunities for students. The future economic health of MGCCC's four-county region depends on many more people getting the necessary skills and credentials to fill open jobs, and MGCCC is at the center of creating this reality.

Even in the face of challenges, MGCCC sees the opportunity that lies ahead for its region, including the rural communities it serves. "We're acutely aware of that rural opportunity: you could change the whole landscape, the whole population, with the right company coming in," said Dr. Erin Riggins, associate vice president of workforce solutions. "That's why we always want to make sure that we're providing the training necessary."

CHAPTER 3

Making the Case

How NOVA Is Transforming into a Jobs-First Hub in Northern Virginia

Furman Haynes

EXECUTIVE SUMMARY

Containing two of four of the richest counties in the country, Northern Virginia is a region blessed with large and fast-growing industries abundant with good-paying jobs. Healthcare, information technology (IT), and cybersecurity have all been growing rapidly in the region, and higher education has been a long-standing priority for Northern Virginia to meet its full economic potential.

However, the wealth present in the region often obscures unequal access to opportunity and concentrated areas of poverty. Northern Virginia Community College (NOVA) sits at the forefront of efforts to ensure economic opportunity is shared more broadly. In a labor market with high concentrations of degrees and high levels of credential requirements, the community college provides the most accessible entry point to higher education, particularly for students from low-income backgrounds.

To achieve this mission, NOVA has embraced a strategy to build more on-ramps into the local economy. Traditionally a transfer-focused institution supporting a relatively young population, NOVA has started to turn its attention toward jobs and workforce. Two of the fastest growing industries in Northern Virginia, IT and healthcare, are what the college calls *lattice industries*—industries with strong sub–bachelor's degree markets in which it is possible to move in multiple directions. To respond, the college is prioritizing creation of short-term programs that culminate in *both* academic credit and a credential with value in the labor market.

Threading the needle between transfer and workforce orientation is a challenging balance for any two-year institution. Yet NOVA is one of the best national examples of a community college with a clear strategy to do both. Through its cloud computing pathway program and others like it, NOVA is building best-in-class models that both respond to growing demands in the region and remove barriers to bachelor's degree attainment, through interventions ranging from guided pathways and automatic enrollment in four-year partners to complete credit articulation, dedicated success coaches, and internships.

The thoughtful deployment of labor market information has been at the center of NOVA's efforts to integrate its workforce and transfer missions. Externally, NOVA's labor market intelligence (LMI) team has become a reputable source of labor market data and workforce insights for the region. The college's expertise in analyzing data and delivering workforce insights helped it build a strategic partnership with the regional chamber of commerce—which in turn has helped in areas related to employer engagement, such as internship recruitment and full-time job placement. LMI has also played a critical role in helping to bring new external resources into the institution to expand proven programs with demonstrated employer demand. Based in part on the strength of its labor market analytics, NOVA received a $5.1 million earmark from the federal government to build a new data center operations program in partnership with the robust and ever-growing NOVA data center industry. Strong labor market data also contributed to NOVA securing $25 million from the State of Virginia to expand its medical registered nurse program and $15 million to build a new skilled trades center.

Meanwhile, internally, LMI has driven many institutional choices, including major investment and curricular decisions. Five years ago, even before Amazon moved to town, the college's data predicted the need for more students trained in cloud computing. Labor market data showed that the demand for tech talent in Northern Virginia was horizontal—it cut across every single industry—and as a result, NOVA built a first-of-its-kind cloud computing associate's degree. In contrast, labor market data have also been used as key input in decisions to shutter programs. For NOVA, the low wages of graduates in its hospitality program were a major factor in closing that program.

The increased focus on creating on-ramps to good jobs in Northern Virginia has also impacted the college's noncredit strategy. In recent years, NOVA has deprioritized recreational and personal interest noncredit courses in favor of job-focused offerings. In addition, the college has leveraged Virginia's FastForward funding initiative to reach more adult learners and subsidize short-term workforce-focused training and credentials in high-demand fields.

Finally, NOVA has been engaged in active efforts to reimagine the delivery of career services across the institution. A recent working group laid out a new vision for career services featuring a "flipped" model. The idea is to front-load career offerings so that students receive the most career support and take more career-focused classes as early as possible. By accelerating career supports, students can acquire skills and credentials early in their academic experience that will still be of value if they stop out. In addition, the career services office is leveraging a "train the trainer" model to scale career coaching college-wide in a resource-constrained environment.

INTRODUCTION

NOVA found itself in the national spotlight in September 2018, when the first batch of students enrolled in its new cloud computing associate's degree program. The demand-driven program, which had been built in partnership with Amazon Web Services, was one of the first cloud computing degrees in the nation offered by a community college and quickly attracted local and national press.[1]

Two months later, more news broke: Amazon announced it would build one of its two HQ2 locations in National Landing, Virginia, barely five miles down the road from NOVA's Alexandria campus.[2] The regional focus on workforce and talent development in the HQ2 application, including the state's $1.1 billion investment in the new Tech Talent Pipeline, was the clear

TABLE 3.1 Northern Virginia Community College quick facts*

Location	Washington-Arlington-Alexandria, DC-VA-MD-WV (Suburban, Mid-Atlantic)
Percentage of county residents who hold a bachelor's degree or above	62.1%
Median household income of county residents	$127,866
Total unduplicated enrollment count of credit and noncredit students	72,798
Percentage credit vs. noncredit	96% credit/4% noncredit
Percentage of full-time vs. part-time students (credit students only)	18% full-time/82% part-time
Percentage of students who received Pell Grants (credit students only)	41%

Sources: College Scorecard, 2021; US Department of Commerce Economics and Statistics Administration, US Census Bureau, US Department of Housing and Urban Development; US Census Bureau, 2020; Northern Virginia Community College; Raj Chetty, John Friedman, Emmanuel Saez, Nicholas Turner, and Danny Yagan, Mobility Report Cards: The Role of Colleges in Intergenerational Mobility, NBER Working Paper No. 23618, 2017.

*Enrollment data represents 2021–2022 numbers, inclusive of credit, noncredit, and dual enrollment students, as provided by Northern Virginia Community College.

differentiator between Northern Virginia and competing regions, according to Amazon.[3] Institutional leaders at NOVA had helped advise the lead applicant, the Virginia Economic Development Partnership, on the proposal. NOVA, with the leadership of Scott Ralls and then Anne Kress, had spent years seeding the ground for an institution-wide focus on workforce. And then, in the span of three months, NOVA found itself in the midst of a national conversation about how to best prepare the skilled workforce of one of the largest technology companies in the world. How would NOVA use this attention to further its institutional objectives?

NOVA was facing a complex set of challenges too. The institution was struggling to reconcile its new workforce vision with its historical niche supporting students in transferring to top colleges and universities in the greater Washington region. NOVA also faced challenges in making job placement a priority for its students given the bachelor's degree–heavy labor market within which it operated. The region's economy is reliant on the federal government and defense industry, which are notorious for rigid degree requirements and other barriers, like security clearances. Even four-year colleges and universities

FIGURE 3.1 NOVA enrollment by race/ethnicity, 2021–2022 academic year

FIGURE 3.2 NOVA enrollment by gender, 2021–2022 academic year

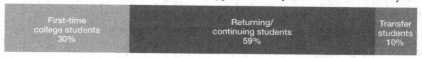

FIGURE 3.3 NOVA students by enrollment type (credit only), 2021–2022 academic year

FIGURE 3.4 NOVA enrollment by age, 2021–2022 academic year

were struggling to produce enough talent to meet employer demand, especially in rapid-growth industries like cybersecurity and healthcare.[4] NOVA was striving to match this demand and prove the value of sub-bachelor's-degree credentials to local employers.

Fast forward to today: NOVA has taken a series of deliberate steps to become an institution that integrates its workforce and transfer missions. NOVA succeeds at encouraging students to seek out sub-bachelor's-degree (or even sub-associate's-degree) credentials with labor market value *and* continue on to bachelor's degree attainment. The community college excels at partnering with employers to build new degree and nondegree offerings. This work started under the leadership of Dr. Scott Ralls, who wrote a strategic plan and launched several initiatives that began to catalyze change within NOVA. As he explained it, NOVA went "from a focus on workforce development as a division of the college to a core purpose of our institution."[5] Ralls's successor as president of NOVA, Anne Kress, is bringing to the table an even more expansive vision for how the institution can support students in achieving economic mobility. President Kress also relies on an experienced group of senior leaders at NOVA, including Steve Partridge, vice president for strategy, research, and workforce innovation; and Dr. Chad Knights, vice president for information and engineering technologies and college computing.

NOVA continues to operate its cloud computing degree in partnership with Amazon and George Mason University. Amazon even published a case study on its website to promote this partnership as a model for other employers and institutions to replicate.[6] NOVA now has a number of distinguishing initiatives, including its LMI team; a new initiative called FastForward, delivering academic credit and labor market credentials to working learners; and additional fundraising capacity. Recently, NOVA also received a $5.1 million earmark from the federal government—the largest federal appropriation to any community college across the country—to build a new data center operations program.[7] While other data center providers participated, including CoreSite, Equinix, Digital Realty, and STACK Infrastructure, the employer partner most heavily involved was Amazon.[8]

Casual observers could attribute the institution's courtship of Amazon to luck, timing, or location. But NOVA's success in establishing itself as a workforce hub in Northern Virginia did not happen overnight. Instead, the institution took a gradual approach to reform that included a deliberate set of choices about institutional priorities. This case study will detail some of the key ingredients that are pivotal to NOVA's success, starting with a deliberate identity transformation that included committed leadership and internal reorganization. This effort was further accelerated by investments in human capital, communications, and resourcing, all of which have enabled the institution to become a powerful example of a community college building multiple pathways from higher education to work.

HOW NOVA IS (SLOWLY) CHANGING ITS CORE IDENTITY

Urban, rural, tech, healthcare: two-year institutions across the country occupy a wide variety of identities. Two in particular elicit the most debate: academic (transfer-focused) and workforce.

NOVA, like many community colleges, has long been a site of debate about the proper balance between these two missions. A *Washington Post* article about NOVA from 1999 details, "The tension between technical education and a more traditional liberal arts education is unavoidable."[9] The article makes the case for retaining a core liberal arts education at NOVA. Over the last decade, through multiple strategic plans and two different college presidents, NOVA has undergone an identity transformation that has expanded beyond a focus on transfer to include workforce. In the process, NOVA is showing what it really takes to build genuine on- and off-ramps between education and work. NOVA's early success with this new integration vision challenges the myth that academic transfer and workforce are mutually exclusive goals incapable of being reconciled within one institution.

A Look at the Regional Context

Founded in 1964, NOVA is the largest public educational institution in Virginia and the second-largest community college in the United States, comprised of more than fifty thousand students, including nearly twenty thousand full-time students, and 2,600 faculty and staff members.[10] Located near Washington, DC, NOVA includes six campuses—Alexandria, Annandale, Loudoun, Manassas, MEC (Springfield), and Woodbridge—along with Reston Educational Center and its online division, NOVA Online. The online division, which existed pre-COVID, now supports around a third of NOVA's student population and has helped limit the institution's enrollment declines during the pandemic to under the 5 percent mark.[11]

For much of its history, NOVA focused on providing transfer-focused academic programs to its relatively young student population. Indeed, NOVA is surrounded by a multitude of prominent four-year institutions: George Mason, Marymount, Howard, Georgetown, George Washington, and Johns Hopkins, to name just a few. As part of the HQ2 announcement, Virginia Tech also announced it would build a new $1 billion innovation campus in Alexandria. Historically, NOVA existed within the greater Washington higher education ecosystem in its defined niche as a well-respected transfer institution to these world-class universities. Workforce wasn't a top priority for NOVA.

There is a notable gap between the highly affluent region in which NOVA sits and the typical NOVA student. NOVA's campuses are located in two of the four richest counties in the country, adjusting for cost of living: Loudoun County (#1 with an adjusted median household income of $126,674) and Fairfax County (#4 with an adjusted median household income of

$103,100).[12] That spread of wealth, however, hides serious concentrated areas of poverty in the region, including "fifteen islands of disadvantage" identified by a new report, *Getting Ahead: The Uneven Opportunity Landscape in Northern Virginia*.[13] NOVA's students are much more likely to come from these marginalized areas than they are to come from the wealthier parts of Northern Virginia: 41 percent of NOVA students are Pell-eligible, for example. NOVA's student population clearly isn't representative of its socioeconomic backyard.

Given the high concentration of degrees in the greater region, NOVA has long been a transfer-focused institution that supports a relatively young population of students through traditional academic pathways. NOVA offers sixty-six two-year degree programs, ten certificate programs, and forty-five career studies certificate programs. In the past, NOVA poured significant resources into building academic transfer pathways to regional institutions like George Mason and others. The institution has now built partnerships with local four-year universities that include guaranteed admissions for NOVA students and common academic pathways. The institution has always prided itself on its academic rigor and quality. NOVA, for example, was recently named a top producer of US Fulbright scholars.[14] NOVA has made this list of top-producing institutions for Fulbright scholars six times since 2009 and has produced twenty-eight Fulbright recipients—the highest number of any community college.

Labor Market Supply and Demand in Northern Virginia

NOVA's emphasis on its students transferring to four-year institutions aligns strategically to the concentration of credentials and local labor market demand in its region: 71 percent of high school graduates (ages twenty-five to sixty-four) hold an associate's degree or higher in Northern Virginia compared to 47 percent nationally.[15]

As the Brookings Institution notes, "The Washington region has one of the most highly educated populations in the country."[16] The supply of credentialed talent isn't the only notable local dynamic. On the demand side, a growing proportion of good jobs in the region require a bachelor's degree. Of all job postings in the Northern Virginia region, 85 percent require a minimum of a bachelor's degree.[17] If we just consider IT jobs, one of the fastest growing job clusters in the region, we see a 40 percent gap between the supply of and demand for bachelor's degree–level human capital.

Despite high levels of educational attainment, there still exist wide discrepancies between the demand and supply of credentials in the region, in part because the fastest growing occupations in the Northern Virginia economy all require a bachelor's degree. The Northern Virginia region has two large and quickly growing industries: (1) healthcare and (2) IT/cybersecurity. Both industries have high levels of credential and degree requirements.

There is some evidence that Virginia is a region that has experienced *degree inflation*, defined as an increase in the number of jobs requiring a four-year degree that previously did not require one. Indeed, jobs like user support specialist, which is the third most populous IT occupation in Northern Virginia, is cited by an Emsi Burning Glass report as one job category with the largest credential difference (21 percent) between current job holders and job requirements. At the very least, as one Organization for Economic Co-operation and Development (OECD) report on Northern Virginia puts it, there is "growing skill intensity within and between occupations."[18] Research from the National Skills Coalition paints a similar picture: "many middle-skill jobs that previously required a high school diploma now require some form of postsecondary education or training."[19] The reality is that NOVA operates in an environment in which credential attainment plays an outsized role. "With a relatively high proportion of post-secondary-intensive occupations, Virginia's economy depends on strengthening the supply of middle and advanced skills," says the OECD report.[20]

A New Vision and Strategic Plan for Nova

NOVA operates within this geographic and economic context. The institution's transformation started with an acknowledgement of its historical identity and a willingness to think beyond its role as a transfer institution. Seven years ago, Scott Ralls and his senior leadership team wrote a new strategic plan—*NOVA Strategic Plan 2017–2023: Pathways to the American Dream*—that included a bold new commitment to a workforce mission:

> NOVA must also more adequately connect job preparation to regional employment needs as suggested by the 21st Century Commission on the Future of Community Colleges. This will entail moving from a focus on workforce development as a division of the college to a core purpose of our institution, offering programs that provide a gateway to regional employment

> "[The college aims to move] from a focus on workforce development as a division of the college to a core purpose of our institution."
>
> —*NOVA Strategic Plan 2017–2023: Pathway to the American Dream*

opportunities, and intensive partnering with employers and organizations to strengthen career development, work-based learning, job placement and other supports that will both enhance the opportunities of our students to participate in a dynamic regional economy and the overall prosperity of the communities that encompass our region.[21]

The move from divisional initiative to college-wide priority was a crucial first step in the ongoing identity transformation at NOVA. Ralls then took a number of steps to execute on this vision, including building new partnerships with employers and a new Labor Market Insights team, both discussed in more detail later in this case study.

President Kress has doubled down on this workforce vision and propelled the institution from adopting a new identity into acting on it. When she arrived in fall 2020, she saw that NOVA "had turned its attention towards workforce but still had a ways to go if it was to build more on-ramps into the local economy."[22] Kress came to her position with clarity into what the institution is and is not with respect to these lofty goals. The question she and her senior leadership team faced was even more daunting than the one facing her predecessor. The institution had a crucial foundation for its broad workforce vision. How would Kress continue this momentum and truly operationalize the vision articulated in the five-year strategic plan—especially for an academic-focused institution in a bachelor's degree–heavy labor market?

Delivering Workforce Insights Through Labor Market Data

NOVA's success is due in large part to key investments made in its internal capacity to analyze labor market data. In 2016, President Ralls hired Steve Partridge as vice president for strategy, research, and workforce innovation. This role was charged with building a team focused on how to operationalize the commitment to workforce outcomes for all students across the institution. One of Partridge's first moves was to build an LMI team that included two data analysts. Since then, the LMI team has greatly increased the capacity of the institution to collect, analyze, and publish labor market data.

An internal labor market insights team helps NOVA play a unique role in collecting data and disseminating powerful reports both internally and externally. The team is prolific: it publishes quarterly State of the Workforce reports that include real-time data on job postings, wages, and skill requirements by industry job; annual workforce briefs that take deep dives into specific high-growth industries like healthcare, business and finance, and IT; and annual county hiring profiles for jurisdiction-specific data from surrounding counties. Also included on the

> "[NOVA has] expertise in crunching data and delivering workforce insights, which is relatively unique compared to other institutions."
>
> *—Julie Coons, President, Northern Virginia Chamber of Commerce*

LMI website are student-facing data on career ladders and pathways into specific industries and interactive dashboards with economic and demographic data. In addition, last year, the NOVA LMI team worked with the Northern Virginia Chamber of Commerce (NVCC) to publish the first ever Northern Virginia Workforce Index, which highlights the state of remote work, hiring and education requirements, and on-the-job training.

Julie Coons, president of NVCC, praises NOVA for its "expertise in crunching data and delivering workforce insights, which is relatively unique compared to other institutions." NOVA's LMI team has become a reputable source of labor market data and workforce insights for the region, according to Coons. By building its capacity in this domain, NOVA has been able to build a strategic partnership with the regional chamber of commerce—which has in turn helped in areas related to employer engagement, like internship recruitment and full-time job placement.[23]

Linking Programs to Employers and College Credit

An internal labor market team also allows the institution to spot gaps between program offerings and fast-growing industries—and then go build new programs in these industries with employers. As Partridge said, "NOVA's role is to manage supply and demand in the workforce system." The institution has begun to use labor market data to make decisions about program openings and closings in the last decade. The LMI team provides historic and forward-looking data about projected job openings and wage growth for a given career path. Some of this data is delivered through the Curriculum Advisory Boards, made up of regional employers who review curricular updates and other program offerings. The NOVA team acknowledges they are still working to improve how these boards function.

NOVA's playbook on opening and closing programs starts with this labor market data: either seeing huge growth in a high-wage job category for which it currently has no program or sluggish growth for a category with an existing program. Chad Knights, vice president for the Information and Engineering Technologies (IET) department, calls this *environmental scanning*. And five years ago, says Partridge, even before Amazon moved to town, NOVA saw the need for more students trained in cloud computing. After all, Northern Virginia has the second largest concentration of tech jobs in the country—and the need for tech talent is horizontal; that is, it cuts across every single industry.

After grounding itself in labor market demand, NOVA then goes to local employers to validate demand and cocreate a new program together. Said Kress, "Employers really drive the new programming and non-degree offerings at the school."

PARTNERSHIP WITH AMAZON WEB SERVICES

Partridge and Knights first began a conversation with Mike Berman and the Amazon Web Services team in 2017, a year prior to any news of HQ2. From the outset, the NOVA team approached the potential partnership with a real learning mindset, understanding that much of the cloud computing training content that AWS had built internally might be shared and leveraged at NOVA. The Aspen Institute's *Workforce Playbook* for community colleges, which features the AWS Cloud Computing associate of applied science (AAS) degree as a best-in-class model, describes why this humble approach works: "These corporations and colleges found that it was more efficient for the companies to map and update curriculum themselves to keep pace with the ever-evolving skills needs for technical jobs. But they rely on the colleges to deliver instruction and consult on pedagogy."[24]

The NOVA team initially set out to integrate some of the cloud training content from AWS into its existing IT and engineering programs within Knight's IET department. Soon, however, they realized they could build out an entirely new degree program. The NOVA team's ability to adapt as the conversation evolved had much to do with having the right people at the table, from academic experts to internal decision-makers to outside experts on the labor market and cloud computing. "They aren't married to a single model

and are willing to adapt to different Amazon initiatives," said Berman from Amazon. He remarked
on the institution's speed and responsiveness, not-
ing, "NOVA has a bias towards action; an ability to
move fast and adjust to the pace of business . . . we
work with them because they have a diverse population of students and are willing to be agile to meet
employers' needs." This ability to move fast wasn't a
given. With its size and diffuse organization structure across six campuses, NOVA had to work hard

> "NOVA has a bias towards action; an ability to move fast and adjust to the pace of business . . . we work with them because they have a diverse population of students and are willing to be agile to meet employers' needs."
>
> —*Mike Berman, Principal of Economic and Workforce Development at Amazon Web Services*

internally to get the right people to the table and respond creatively to get this
program up and running. Soon, it had built the first cloud computing degree
in the nation offered by a community college, a four-year pathway from NOVA
to George Mason that Higher Ed Dive deemed "the partnership of the year."[25]

NOVA continues to operate its cloud computing AAS program, which
now exists as part of a four-year pathway program called ADVANCE that
includes both George Mason and Amazon Web Services as partners. AD-
VANCE has been noted by many as a best-in-class transfer model that re-
moves barriers for students that typically prevent them from securing a
bachelor's degree in a high-demand field like cloud computing. The guided
pathway model includes automatic enrollment in George Mason, complete
credit articulation, dedicated success coaches, and internships. About AD-
VANCE, Partridge said: "[The program is] helping students get through an
associate degree and then bachelor's degree as cheaply and quickly as possible
before entering into the workforce." In short, the program is removing many
of the inequitable barriers that prevent students from ever achieving a bachelor's degree, while also ensuring they get at least an associate's degree if they
decide to enter the workforce at any point.

PARTNERSHIP WITH GOODWIN LIVING

NOVA has seen other successes in building programs that match employer
demand and deconstruct the four-year degree to allow more students to access in-demand fields. As President Kress notes about the two fastest growing industries in Northern Virginia, "Both IT and healthcare have a strong
sub-baccalaureate market, so we need to build on-ramps at every level. These

are lattice industries where it is possible to move in sideways directions." Kress has a clear definition of what she means by *on-ramps at every level*. The key, for NOVA at least, is creating short-term programs that culminate with both academic credit and a valuable labor market credential, propelling people into the workforce in a middle-income job while not precluding that they return to NOVA or another institution to complete a degree.

Take the Advanced Certified Nursing Assistant (Advanced CNA) program as just one example. The shortage of qualified nurses in Northern Virginia has been a growing source of concern for policymakers, healthcare employers, and workforce providers. According to Kress, NOVA has seen increased demand and willingness to pay from local employers across different roles on the nursing career ladder. NOVA had worked with Goodwin Living, a provider and operator of aging services in Northern Virginia, for many years as one of its clinical site partners for its CNA program. Through this existing partnership, Goodwin Living worked with NOVA to develop a curriculum for the Advanced CNA certification, a state certification from the Virginia Board of Nursing. The course schedule was customized to allow students to maintain their jobs as CNAs while completing the certification. NOVA worked with Goodwin Living staff and subject matter experts to create a flexible six-week program that allowed full-time CNAs at Goodwin Living to attain the Advanced CNA credential.

Josh Bagley, administrator at Goodwin Living, cites NOVA's adaptability as its most powerful trait as an academic partner, echoing the comments of the Amazon team. Students are the ultimate beneficiaries of this innovation. CNAs have been historically immobile in the healthcare labor market; many view the role as a dead-end job. With this certification, students are able to earn higher wages and move into middle management positions. Christy Martinez, who previously completed two years at George Mason before leaving school due to family circumstances, says the Advanced CNA program has helped her learn how to work with and manage people: "I've moved to a higher position in my job because of this program. I'm now the lead [CNA] responsible for training other people my age."

At this point, the college does not build labor market data into its internal accountability or review process. The LMI team still is able to provide data to curriculum advisory boards and to academic program leads, both of which use these data when making curricular decisions. But the use of data is still ad hoc and requires presidential approval. Kress and her leadership team opted to close the hospitality program, however, given its historically low wages. Said Kress, "We closed the hospitality program even though everyone loved it because these graduates weren't making any more money than someone with a high school degree." Shuttering programs using labor market data can be one of the most difficult and controversial decisions for a community college president. In this case, Kress found her faculty were largely supportive of this decision. But NOVA still has room to improve on institutionalizing the use of labor market data for program expansion or termination decisions.

While the bulk of NOVA's program offerings still focus on traditional academic pathways, the institution also has taken numerous steps to include a more explicit focus on workforce in its noncredit programs. NOVA has re-focused its non-credit-bearing courses on industry credentials with proven labor market value. *Noncredit courses* are any short-term program offerings, usually two to ten weeks in length, that end in a certificate that doesn't link to academic credit within the institution. From 2019 to 2020, NOVA awarded 28,756 associate's transfer degrees, 6,460 associate's workforce degrees, and 1,283 certificates. NOVA's noncredit programs historically focused on personal interest microcourses for adults (e.g., cooking classes). A Rutgers study on noncredit programs describes NOVA's transformation since then:[26] "About five years ago, Northern Virginia Community College also began to focus their offerings on upskilling and reskilling and to pare down recreational courses and programs for seniors, including many personal interest courses and short one-day programs like walking tours. As a result, NOVA's noncredit enrollments were reduced from over 20,000 per year to about 6,000 to 8,000 per year, but the college's mission is now more clearly to meet skills needs."

By reducing the number of extraneous noncredit programs, the institution has been able to focus on building more high-quality noncredit programs that lead to good jobs. A cursory scan of the Continuing Education page on NOVA's website shows that the number of personal interest courses has dropped dramatically. In their place are numerous different short-term classes in IT, cybersecurity, and business management.

SHORT-TERM TRAINING AND CREDENTIALS

The build-out of nondegree pathways with labor market value is aided by a new funding source: FastForward, a new statewide funding program in Virginia that subsidizes short-term workforce focused training and credentials. For the first time in state history, qualifying students can access financial assistance and aid for six to twelve weeks of noncredit workforce training and acquire an industry credential. At NOVA, short-term courses that qualify for FastForward funding include CompTIA A+, Nurse Aide Preparation (CNA), or AWS Cloud Practitioner. This state policy is a crucial enabler of program innovation that allows an institution like NOVA to integrate its workforce and academic mission.

The typical age of a NOVA student participating in FastForward is thirty years old, almost a decade older than the median student across the institution, who is about twenty-one years old. Why does age matter? The institution is proving it can build short-term programs that serve adults while also ensuring these programs articulate into the credit side of the house. Another example of this work is a new IT apprenticeship program built in partnership with AT&T.[27] After building this apprenticeship model that led to industry-recognized credentials, Chad Knights in the IET department realized the program wouldn't fully realize the institutional vision that integrates academic and workforce missions unless he linked it to academic credit. After working through some hesitancy both within his team and in the academic affairs department, he convinced them to use the *credit for prior learning* (CPL; a.k.a. *prior learning assessment*) mechanism. The American Council on Education defines CPL as "academic credit granted for demonstrated college-level equivalencies gained through learning experiences outside of the college classroom."[28] The academic affairs team now has a full-time staff member devoted to CPL.

NOVA is clearly working hard to link academic credit to these workforce programs. When asked what "big plays" NOVA will pursue in the next five years, Kress mentions two: (1) shorter, accelerated workforce programs with demonstrated labor market value and (2) better linkages to academic credit for these programs. She says that more high-quality workforce programs will answer the needs of today's students. "The pandemic showed that time is of the essence for people; time is almost more important than money for people. The opportunity costs are huge," said Kress. To ensure those programs aren't dead ends for students, Kress emphasizes the importance of the second goal, saying NOVA can do a better job of automating the task of recognizing credit for prior learning. Much attention is being paid to this topic in the sector nationally, as Kress surely is aware. By pairing these two goals, she and NOVA are fulfilling the vision of an institution with a dual focus on jobs *and* creating more pathways into further education and training for its students. This vision and execution roadmap serves as an example for any institution claiming it wants to build more on-ramps and off-ramps between higher education and the labor market.

Reimagining Career Services

NOVA has also taken meaningful steps to expand and redesign its career services offerings to students. In 2020, President Kress convened a working group to reimagine career services across the institution. The working group published a report that laid out a new vision for career services, defined by a "flipped" model in which students receive most career support and take most career-focused classes as early as possible in their journey at the college. The model relies on a clear student progression model (with steps for connection, entry, progression, and completion). Many students, for example, take a Career Leadership and Readiness Institute class, a for-credit class that includes a variety of career-focused workshops. Front-loading the career supports offered to students means that students can receive credentials with labor market value early in their academic experience in case they stop out. Going forward, NOVA is considering using a creative metric to determine how well it is succeeding at this flipped model: how long its academic students stay in the general studies program versus choosing to commit to a specific major or field.

NOVA is also tinkering with its career advising model. As a large, decentralized institution with over fifty thousand students and only six dedicated career services team members, the institution is well aware that it won't be able to reach all students unless it institutionalizes an approach to supporting students' career development. That starts with using technology: the Office of Career Services uses Career Connection, powered by Symplicity, to offer students a one-stop shop for career exploration, resume-building, job postings, and more. As part of their core curriculum, most students are required to take a personal development class that involves a career module and online personal assessment tool. NOVA benefits from supportive state policy here

---

Guaranteed Interviews

NOVA's career services team is now piloting an innovative Guaranteed Interviews program for its students. Participating employers commit to a screening interview for those who successfully complete a program that includes various career supports, like resume preparation and mock interviews. Students nearing the completion of an applied degree get the opportunity to interview with local employers, exposing them to a professional interview process and helping them expand their network. Employers, meanwhile, get access to NOVA students with credentials and employable skills in dynamic, high-demand fields. And many students, with the training and support of this program, are already getting jobs.

---

too: a decade ago, the Virginia Community College System (VCCS) launched VA Wizard in 2009, an online portal that helps young people consider various careers and further education and training options by taking into account their skills, interests, and values.

Aware of the constraints of its large student population, the Office of Career Services is now leveraging a "train the trainer" model to scale its career-coaching model college-wide. The team is working with the LMI team to ensure that labor market data and appropriate guidance on career coaching reach the various other adults (e.g., academic counselors, professors, and others) who interact with students every day. This kind of approach is crucially necessary for an institution of NOVA's size.

NOVA'S DISTINGUISHING ENABLERS: ORGANIZATIONAL DESIGN, HUMAN CAPITAL, FUNDRAISING, AND COMMUNICATION

Four key institutional priorities distinguish NOVA's success to date:

1. User-centered organizational design
2. Forward-looking human capital strategy
3. Diversified resourcing
4. Branding as a regional economic hub

User-Centered Organizational Design

Large institutions like NOVA with diffuse reporting lines and decentralized resources must be willing to experiment with their internal organization. NOVA historically has been heavily decentralized; all credit and noncredit programs have typically been administered separately by each of the six campuses. Given its institutional makeup, NOVA has had to find novel ways to organize itself to operationalize this new workforce vision.

In fall 2020, as previously mentioned, Kress convened a working group of faculty and academic counselors and challenged them to reimagine career services at the institution. Previously, career services were delivered separately by each of the six campuses, leading to duplication of efforts like employer engagement and confusion from students who cross-registered across multiple campuses. The working group produced a culminating report that called for more resources devoted to this institutional reform effort, but the report lacked any clear blueprint for what the institution needed to do internally to accomplish such change. Kress went back to the working group and asked for a clear implementation plan that would include the career services team being more closely connected to the workforce team—"since we were the group closest to employers," said Partridge. By March 2021, a plan was approved to centralize all career services under Partridge and his workforce division.

Most community colleges have one employer engagement staff member sitting within the career services team. NOVA took a different approach: Kress and Partridge brought the career services staff into the workforce division responsible for employer engagement and labor market data. This move helped institutionalize the college-wide focus on career development. By coordinating college-wide workforce programming and using technology to deliver new virtual events during COVID-19, NOVA found it was able to dramatically increase the level of student engagement at career-related events, panels, and so on.

This reorganization also included creating a new Office of Strategic Insights that merged the Office of Institutional Research (OIR), responsible for all student data, with the LMI team. This internal redesign helped connect internal assets and information flows. OIR had an existing license with labor market data provider Emsi Burning Glass that it had never used, for instance. With this new structure, the OIR staff handling student data and decisions about program offerings now sit in the same office as those staff with expertise in analyzing labor market data. The new Office of Strategic Insights has become a central source of data at the institution, providing quarterly reports on student achievement and labor market projections to internal stakeholders, including academic teams and curriculum advisory boards.

Organizational redesign has also helped empower Knights to create a highly innovative and successful academic program within his IET department. In 2017, Ralls tried to call an internal meeting to respond to demand from IT employers. Over twenty different people from across all six campuses and other parts of the institution showed up. Ralls questioned how such a decentralized group within the institution would ever respond to employer needs. He decided to centralize the academic departments into one dedicated unit focused on IT and engineering technology. Ralls tapped Knights to lead the IET department, which became one of the first academic programs to be operated centrally in this way at NOVA. With the new, streamlined department, Knights now has the resources and flexibility to build programs at the speed of business. Shortly after the IET department was reorganized, Amazon came knocking on NOVA's door, asking if the institution would partner to develop a cloud computing degree. Knights stepped in to lead the NOVA team that built a new cloud computing degree program with Amazon in a matter of months. With more centralized resources and decision-making power, Knights was able to quickly build an academic program from scratch using much of the Amazon Web Services cloud computing training content. Intentional organizational design explains much of the agility that Mike Berman from Amazon Web Services cites as being a crucial component of NOVA's attractiveness as an institutional partner.

Knights and his team operate a number of other highly successful programs within the IET department, many of which are unique for an academic department within a community college. Seeing the need for additional soft skills support for his students, Knights helped build the Career Readiness and Leadership Institute. The institute's programs, which include workshops on everything from obtaining industry certification and security clearances to mock interviews, have now been scaled across NOVA. Knights has also raised money from the National Science Foundation to extend the reach of NOVA's K–12 STEM outreach program, NOVA SySTEMic. This group has been working with school districts throughout NOVA's service area to promote STEM education and provide exposure to careers in STEM fields.[29] Knights also remains in close communication with Partridge and the LMI team within the workforce division to ensure they keep an eye on fast-growing technology job clusters. In addition to the AWS cloud computing degree, Knights also built a new data intelligence program for active-duty Marine Corps members.[30] The new course of study focuses on data analytics, machine learning, and artificial intelligence.

Forward-Looking Human Capital Strategy

Chad Knights and the IET department are exemplary for their ability to build new initiatives that better match the needs of both employers and students. Knights is cited by many for his leadership within the institution. And he has been recognized externally too: in 2020, Amazon selected Knights in its faculty cohort for the AWS Educate Cloud Ambassador Program.[31] Knights is just one example of NOVA's laser focus on bringing in high-quality talent to lead parts of the institution. Said President Kress, "It comes down to people and always does . . . You can buy all the labor management data or labor market information data that you want, but if you don't have people who are invested, then you are missing the secret sauce."

NOVA has been able to recruit high-caliber talent to lead much of the work to transform the institution into a jobs-first hub. Leadership at the top is indispensable, which starts with the president's office. Kress is viewed internally and externally as a strong leader who balances vision and execution. She is recognized especially for her ability to manage external affairs, including bringing in new funding sources and helping advocate for NOVA within the broader regional ecosystem (discussed in subsequent sections). Before Kress, Ralls was seen by many as one of the most forward-looking community college presidents in the country. The Amazon team noted that he was involved personally in many of the conversations that led to the strong partnership between the two entities.

Talented individuals at the helm helped the community college build crucial partnerships with external partners like employers. Mike Berman from Amazon notes that "NOVA is successful in large part because of the networks of Steve and Chad," referring to Partridge and Knights. Partridge has served in his role since 2016 and is focused on creating a demand-driven workforce development system. Previously, he served as president and CEO of Charlotte Works, the workforce development board for Charlotte and Mecklenburg County. For an institution endeavoring to be a regional workforce hub, much of the work becomes highly relational in nature. As Knights said, "You need real connections to employers, not just labor market data." Partridge, Knights, Kress, and Ralls have all built intentional personal relationships across the external ecosystem.

NOVA's explicit focus on investing in its own internal talent pool is also evident in its focus on building in-house expertise in analyzing labor market data. "You can buy all of the labor market data you want; but if you don't have people invested in these programs . . . it's not going to happen," said Kress.

Diversified Resourcing

NOVA has also refocused on bringing in more external resources to the institution, thanks in large part to Kress. While NOVA is relatively well-funded by the State of Virginia, the institution historically has underperformed peer institutions in winning grants from private foundations, the State of Virginia, and the federal government. NOVA's funding policy environment is mixed at best. The state does provide performance-based funding on graduation metrics for associate's degrees. But state funding includes no weights based on the cost of delivering such a program, so schools have no incentive to build programs that are more expensive to operate (e.g., healthcare), despite labor market demand. VCCS does not allow institutions to develop any additional fees for students participating in more expensive programs. Moreover, Fairfax County has never pursued any municipal bond financing for its local institutions.

Given these challenges, fundraising was a key priority for Anne Kress when she became president of NOVA in fall 2020. She saw this as the "unfinished part: How do we invest in NOVA to ensure we can continue to build programs and deliver to partners?" She has proved adept at leveraging her position to bring in outside philanthropic and state dollars. Kress starts with making a compelling case about NOVA's value proposition as an institution: "There is a huge need for talent and there's also an incredible need to diversify the talent pool—so this is a perfect moment to have conversations with businesses . . . to have conversations with the state . . . or with a federal agency, and say: 'OK, we've got a plan, if you can invest in us, we can grow that workforce, we can diversify that talent pool.'"

The results speak for themselves: more resources translating to more programs that are meeting employer demand in high-growth areas. In just under two years at the helm, Kress has identified the funding and initiated the process of launching or expanding three new programs: data center operations, skilled trades, and healthcare. As previously mentioned, NOVA received a $5.1 million earmark from the federal government, the largest appropriation to a community college in the country, to build a new data center operations program. NOVA will revamp part of an old building on its Woodbridge campus to build a mock data center that will allow young people to get hands-on experience in data center operations, a fast-growing "blue-collar tech" job category. Amazon Web Services, along with the other members of the Data Center Coalition—a group of data center owners that operates nationally—is eager to hire graduates and will work with NOVA to build the program. In addition, NOVA just received $40 million from the State of Virginia, $25 million of which will go toward expanding its medical RN program and $15 million of which will go toward building a new skilled trades center. For both new buildings, Kress and her leadership team looked closely at the labor market data from the LMI team to ensure that there is demonstrated demand for these programs. In addition to clear employer demand, NOVA has seen huge student demand for its RN program; currently, over six hundred students apply to the nursing program annually, which has a capacity of approximately only eighty students. The new funding and building will help expand this program—and, in doing so, meet both student and employer demand.

Branding as a Regional Economic Hub

NOVA's public reputation, sitting mere miles from the nation's capital, enjoys the benefit of proximity. Previous governors and even sitting US presidents have signed bills into law on its campus.[32] And of course, the First Lady, Dr. Jill Biden, still teaches there. Still, according to Anne Kress, for many years the public's view of NOVA has been narrow, seeing it only as a transfer institution to the region's many four-year colleges and universities. Policymakers, employers, and other leaders shaping the economic development and workforce strategies within the region did not see NOVA as a core asset. Said Kress,

"It was clear to me when I got here, despite the best efforts of the institution and all the great work that Scott [Ralls] did, that employers were still looking past NOVA to try to find their solutions. So, one of my strategic imperatives . . . is to make sure that NOVA is always in the conversation."

President Kress has made it a priority to put NOVA on the proverbial map with respect to its role as a regional workforce hub. She has a keen sense of the broader higher education and workforce ecosystem in the greater Washington region—and what role NOVA should play within it. There are numerous employer groups focused on workforce and talent development in the region, including the Greater Washington Partnership, NVCC, Connected DMV, and the Northern Virginia Technology Council, to name but a few. Kress has ensured that NOVA has a seat at these tables of CEOs and decision-makers who talk about regional workforce and talent dynamics.

Kress has been intentional about joining as many of these groups herself as possible. When the Greater Washington Board of Trade started a new group focused on post-COVID economic recovery called Connected DMV, Kress ensured she would be able to join the Connected DMV Strategic Renewal Task Force with other regional leaders. She also sits on the boards of NVCC, the Northern Virginia Technology Council, and the Economic Club of Washington. Partridge and Knights play similarly important roles in external relations. Partridge notes that Kress has challenged and empowered her leadership team to devote face time and energy to getting involved in these regional workforce conversations.

NOVA plays a unique role in workforce advocacy in the region, raising pressure among employers to hire more two-year or certificate students through one-on-one conversations, economic reports, and other means. First, NOVA leadership has taken it upon itself to use its newfound seat at the regional workforce table to advocate that employers expand their hiring requirements to be inclusive of two-year or even sub-associate's degrees. Earlier this year, for example, Kress found herself at a table of regional CEOs who were complaining about the Great Resignation and the cost of high turnover. She pointed out that part of the problem lay with the narrow and costly talent acquisition practices of their companies, asking, "How sustainable are your expensive hiring practices?"

> "One of my strategic imperatives is to make sure that NOVA is always in the conversation."
>
> —*Dr. Anne Kress, President, NOVA*

Julie Coons, president of NVCC, sees NOVA playing an important role as a "good public advocate for the broad range of types of people in that workforce including adults and non-degreed individuals." As previously mentioned, Coons and NVCC worked with NOVA to publish the Workforce Index. In addition to building its brand as an institution with labor market expertise, reports like these also allow NOVA to pursue a subtle kind of advocacy in speaking to employers about the future of degrees and hiring requirements. "Regional businesses generally maintain a conventional approach to education, training, and professional development—yet, now is the perfect opportunity for employers to expand talent pipelines through alternate means, such as apprenticeships."[33]

NOVA also uses media and other PR tools to build momentum for its initiatives. NOVA leveraged the opportunity presented by the announcement of Amazon's HQ2 to build its brand as an institution capable of responding to employer needs. An information technology workforce brief summarizes the ripple effects: "Ever since Amazon announced that a major part of its HQ2 operations would be located in northern Virginia, the region's profile as a national tech hub has skyrocketed. Even before Amazon's announcement, the information technology sector in the Washington D.C. metropolitan area had been experiencing substantial growth, with northern Virginia at its core. As Amazon ramps up hiring in the coming years, and as other technology companies inevitably follow in its wake, the challenges associated with finding talent in such a competitive labor market will only continue to grow."[34]

Chad Knights's entrepreneurial drive to create new programs also extends to communications; press releases go out frequently from his team about a new program or event. In 2019, for example, students in NOVA's cloud computing associate's degree program sat on a panel for Amazon Web Services' Public Sector Summit.[35]

A final communications and advocacy lever NOVA employs is its convening power. The new Advanced CNA program with Goodwin Living, described previously, originated when NOVA convened leaders of nursing homes and other long-term care facilities. The outcome of the meeting was a realization that these employers' talent-retention problems might be solved by investing in their own employees. Consequently, the Advanced CNA program was born, with NOVA in a key role as its academic partner.

Many community colleges face a classic chicken-and-egg puzzle. Employers have to see your institution as a reliable partner—but how can they do that if you can't convince any employer to be the first to partner with you? NOVA has leveraged its geographic assets and investments in human capital to attract attention to the institution and demonstrate its capabilities as a responsive partner. As one report summarized, "community colleges, in general, and NOVA, in particular, have much broader public recognition" than they once did.[36]

CONCLUSION

How can community colleges remain relevant in the twenty-first-century labor market? For NOVA, this question looks a lot like another one: How can an institution focused historically on academic and transfer students evolve to drive economic success for a broader set of learners? NOVA is exemplary for the way it is evolving in a sustainable and intentional manner. A debate among pundits has focused on the purpose of higher education, which includes a growing number of critiques of the "college-for-all" paradigm within which transfer institutions like NOVA operated. Think pieces have called for more on-ramps and off-ramps into well-paying jobs, without acknowledging the many constraints—historical inertia, stakeholder expectations, and internal push back—that prevent this laddered model from being built overnight.

Many question whether building a community college that seamlessly integrates with the labor market at multiple stages is really possible. NOVA, despite its past reputation as a traditional transfer-focused institution, is a powerful example of how an institution can take meaningful steps toward realizing this vision.

NOVA has made the case to its stakeholders, both internally and externally, that a broader focus on workforce outcomes is the right north star for the institution. The institution is leveraging this historical moment, which includes massive forces like a global pandemic, the Great Resignation, and growing corporate attention to building a diverse workforce, to enact change. Responding to this moment requires building a case for community colleges to be an integral part of any effective workforce system that truly meets the needs of learners, workers, and employers.

Anne Kress understands this dynamic better than almost anyone: "You have to build a compelling case that helps folks understand why investing in you and in your students benefits them . . . because at the end of the day it's still a business case—and that's what we've started doing."

CHAPTER 4

Trusted Partner

How Pima Community College
Powers the Economic Development Ecosystem

Rachel Boroditsky

EXECUTIVE SUMMARY

In many ways, the population of the Greater Tucson region and Southern Arizona epitomizes the concept of "new majority learners." As a majority-minority Hispanic-Serving Institution of over thirty-three thousand non-credit and credit students, Pima Community College (a.k.a. Pima) is focused intently on connecting the increasingly diverse population of Pima County to economic mobility. By putting access to jobs at the core of its mission, Pima has enhanced its value proposition for its students, the local economy, and its surrounding community.

Prior to Chancellor Lee Lambert taking on leadership of the college in 2013, Pima struggled to meet the needs of the college's majority working learner population and regional employers. According to interviews, employers found it difficult to navigate Pima's uncoordinated and complex ecosystem of workforce development efforts. At the same time, Pima faced financial pressures due to reductions in state funding and declining enrollments.[1] To top it off, the Higher Learning Commission had just placed Pima on probation.[2]

Over the past decade, Pima has undergone a dramatic transformation to better serve its learners, community, and employers. Chancellor Lambert put workforce and economic development at the top of the college's strategic priorities, and the institution implemented a strategy and paradigm across the college that would align its resources toward advancing its economic mobility mission.

At the center of Pima's strategy is a priority on providing working learners the flexibility they need to succeed. Pima has promoted the development of multiple, flexible pathways across the full spectrum of education and training, ranging from career-focused high school and adult basic education programs to micropathways, certificates, and degrees. All learners can choose between fully online, hybrid, or in-person programs. Pima has also expanded *stackable credentials*—credentials that can be accumulated over time and help workers advance along career ladders in industries. In addition, during the pandemic, the college also developed and launched new *micropathways*, or fast-track programs. Prioritizing stackability, these fast-track programs focus on allowing learners to upgrade their skills quickly and then transition into an in-demand role in the labor market.

In addition, Pima is increasingly blurring the lines between credit and noncredit learners. The college has made a significant investment in a noncredit registration system that integrates with its data warehouse so that that the college can understand outcomes and successes for all learners, not just those in for-credit programs. In addition, leadership created a revamped central employer-facing unit, responsible for all business partnerships, whether the program is credit or noncredit. The college recognized that its internal silos detracted from meeting the needs of employers looking for talent. In addition, the creation of a one-stop shop for workforce removed disincentives to collaboration with academic departments that had been posed by previous revenue-generation requirements.

Pima also is putting applied learning at the center of its strategy. Remarkably, the college is now committed to ensuring that 100 percent of its learners have a work-based learning experience during their time at the college—both credit and noncredit learners. To achieve this vision, Pima's leaders are expanding and scaling work-based learning opportunities ranging from microinternships and job shadowing to internships and apprenticeships.

Externally, **Pima prioritizes being industry-facing and employer-friendly.** The college's ambitious new center of excellence model, supported by $65 million in new funding from bonds, is an example of successful engagement of employer partners. The six new centers, spanning the region's priority industries, are applied technology, healthcare, information technology/cybersecurity, public safety and security, arts and humanities, and hospitality and tourism. These centers feature state-of-the-art facilities and programs jointly conceived and defined by a series of regional industry summits with over 120 local employers. The college is also focused on ensuring that its employer relations are forward-looking. Pima recently created a $1 million innovation seed fund to help incubate new industry training models in the region.

Of course, none of this would be possible without a concerted focus on the supports needed to keep students enrolled and help them be successful on the job. Making education accessible and sustainable for the county's residents has been a prime area for attention. Pima has rolled out new ways to keep costs as low as possible for learners, ranging from efforts to make course materials free to matched savings scholarship programs that can supplement Pell Grants to prior learning assessments that can reduce credit requirements.

As the pandemic recovery unfolds, Pima is well-positioned to build on these reforms and expand its role as a good jobs engine for the region. Prior investments in work-based experiences and flexibility for working learners provide a strong foundation for Pima to embody the increasing responsiveness demanded from higher education in this competitive labor market. The Pima experience provides a compelling model for community colleges.

INTRODUCTION

Located in Southern Arizona, Pima Community College is the only community college for Pima County. Pima is a Hispanic-Serving Institution and primarily serves working adults. In 2021, over thirty-three thousand credit and noncredit learners were enrolled at Pima.[3] Before Chancellor Lee Lambert joined Pima in 2013, the college struggled to meet the needs of its majority working learner population and regional employers. According to interviews, employers found it difficult to navigate Pima's uncoordinated and complex ecosystem of workforce development efforts. At the same time, Pima faced financial pressures due to reductions in state funding and declining

TABLE 4.1 Pima Community College quick facts*

Location	Tucson, AZ (Southwest, Urban)
Percentage of county residents who hold a bachelor's degree or above	33.6%
Median household income of county residents	$55,023
Total unduplicated enrollment count of credit and noncredit students	33,993
Percentage credit vs. noncredit	82% credit/18% noncredit
Percentage of full-time vs. part-time students (credit students only)	29% full-time/71% part-time
Percentage of students who received Pell Grants (credit students only)	57%
Percentage of students from the bottom 40% of the income distribution (credit students only)	36%

Sources: College Scorecard, 2021; US Department of Commerce Economics and Statistics Administration, US Census Bureau, US Department of Housing and Urban Development; US Census Bureau, 2020; Pima Community College; Raj Chetty, John Friedman, Emmanuel Saez, Nicholas Turner, and Danny Yagan, Mobility Report Cards: The Role of Colleges in Intergenerational Mobility, NBER Working Paper No. 23618, 2017.

*Enrollment data represents 2021–2022 numbers, inclusive of credit, noncredit, and dual enrollment students, as provided by Pima Community College.

enrollments.[4] To top it off, the Higher Learning Commission had just placed Pima on probation.[5]

Over the past decade, Pima has undergone a dramatic transformation to better serve its learners, community, and employers. After Lambert became Pima's chancellor, workforce development rose to the top of Pima's strategic priorities. Pima integrated a workforce development paradigm throughout the college and aligned its resources to advance its workforce goals. Through innovative industry partnerships and flexible education and career pathways, Pima has since established itself as a driver of economic development in the region. As the US emerges from the COVID-19 pandemic, Pima continues to improve upon ways to meet the needs of its learners, community, and employers.

The Growing Arizona Economy

Pima County is home to just over one million people,[6] with Tucson as the county seat where most residents live. Over twenty thousand employers serve the labor market in Pima County[7] and help contribute to a diverse economy.

FIGURE 4.1 Pima enrollment by race/ethnicity, 2021–2022 academic year

FIGURE 4.2 Pima enrollment by gender, 2021–2022 academic year

FIGURE 4.3 Pima students by enrollment type (credit only), 2021–2022 academic year

FIGURE 4.4 Pima enrollment by age, 2021–2022 academic year

In 2020, the three largest industries (healthcare, retail, and accommodation and food services) represented approximately 46 percent of private employment.[8] Pima County experienced a 0.8 percent annualized percentage growth in private employment between 2010 and 2020, driven by transportation and warehousing, healthcare, manufacturing, and administrative services industries (see Table 4.2).[9] Aerospace is also one of Pima's core industries. Raytheon, Davis-Monthan Air Force Base, Caterpillar, and the University of Arizona are among the region's largest employers.[10]

Pima County residents are slightly older than residents in the nation overall, and Pima County's population has grown more slowly over the last ten years. Pima County's socioeconomic and ethnic demographics differ from the nation overall: the median household income in Pima County is $55,023,[11] which is lower than the national median of $64,996.[12] In addition, Pima County has approximately double the proportion of residents who identify as Hispanic/Latino compared to the US as a whole (37.8 percent[13] versus 18.5 percent[14]).

Considering these demographics, Pima realized it needed to change the way it served the community. College stakeholders highlighted that Pima needed to prioritize upskilling and reskilling working learners given the

TABLE 4.2 Pima County private employment by industry sector

Industry	Employment (2010)	Employment (2020)	Numeric growth (2010–2020)	Annualized percentage growth (2010–2020)
Total private employment	271,264	292,347	21,083	0.8%
Healthcare and assistance	53,347	60,811	7,464	1.3%
Retail trade	39,644	40,341	697	0.2%
Accommodation and food services	33,564	31,875	(1,689)	–0.5%
Administrative and waste services	24,491	27,622	3,131	1.2%
Manufacturing	23,979	27,290	3,311	1.3%
Professional and technical services	18,521	17,948	(573)	–0.3%
Construction	14,975	17,779	2,804	1.7%
Transportation and warehousing	5,953	14,075	8,122	9.0%
Other services, except public administration	10,589	10,658	69	0.1%
Finance and insurance	11,588	10,321	(1,267)	–1.2%
Wholesale trade	8,045	6,723	(1,322)	–1.8%
Real estate and rental and leasing	5,910	6,156	246	0.4%
Educational services	4,437	5,707	1,270	2.5%
Information	4,313	4,941	628	1.4%
Arts, entertainment, and recreation	4,513	4,024	(489)	–1.1%
Utilities	2,065	2,059	(6)	0.0%
Mining, quarrying, and oil and gas extraction	1,815	1,843	28	0.2%

Industry	Employment (2010)	Employment (2020)	Numeric growth (2010–2020)	Annualized percentage growth (2010–2020)
Management of companies and enterprises	2,804	1,460	(1,344)	−6.3%
Agriculture, forestry, fishing, and hunting	623	603	(20)	−0.3%
Industry unclassified	88	111	23	2.3%

Sources: Bureau of Labor Statistics, Quarterly Census of Employment and Wages, 2010–2020 Annualized Employees in Private NAICS Industries in Pima County, AZ; tables generated using data.census.gov; see https://data.bls.gov/PDQWeb/en, accessed May 2022.

combination of the county's older population and stagnating number of high school graduates. In addition, stakeholders called out Pima's need to serve *new majority learners*—that is, learners who have been historically underserved and underrepresented—given the county's diverse community demographics. Therefore, Pima needed to better align its programs with employer demands and provide flexibility and support to help learners succeed.

PIMA'S TRANSFORMATION

When Lee Lambert was recruited from Shoreline Community College, located in Washington State, to become Pima's chancellor in 2013, Pima was in trouble. The regional accrediting association had placed it on probation for a variety of fiscal and educational problems. A combination of reductions in state funding and enrollment declines had created a fiscal crisis demanding radical action. And Lambert quickly learned from his initial conversations with business leaders that they found it difficult to collaborate with the college.

Consequently, Lambert closed one of what had been six campuses and sold off its buildings. Each campus had formerly had its own president and administrative hierarchy. In two stages, Lambert consolidated administrative

> "When Lambert became chancellor in 2013, we were at rock bottom. Not only were we on probation, but we were facing a huge budget deficit. Big changes would have to be made, and in a hurry."
>
> —Dr. Sylvia Lee, Former Pima Board Chair

structures so that today there is one president, David Dore, to whom the five campuses report.

Perhaps the second most important administrative decision Lambert made was to appoint a new vice president for workforce development and strategic partnerships, Ian Roark, and designate him as the single point of contact for the employer community

When Lambert first toured Pima, he remembers thinking there was an opportunity to revitalize the college's relationships with industry partners and reestablish Pima as a driver of the region's workforce development agenda. Upon starting at Pima, Lambert outlined a vision for the college that focused on addressing five gaps, including the skills gap, to revitalize regional workforce development.[15]

To tackle the skills gap, Lambert wanted to empower Pima's workforce development division and transform the culture around workforce development at Pima. He felt a sense of urgency to "get the right people in the right places, align policies, procedures, and resources and track progress in realtime." Lambert knew he needed support from the board, faculty, and staff to succeed. He shared the five gaps with the board and maintained constant communication to ensure board member buy-in.

In addition, Lambert sought feedback from the rest of the college. He engaged faculty and staff through office hours, one-on-one meetings, and faculty meals. The chancellor also established a framework that detailed Pima's expectations for successful leaders, including a focus on workforce development. Pima's leaders cascaded these expectations throughout the college and incorporated them into the hiring process and performance management system.

Pima's leadership transformed the college by making workforce development one of Pima's top strategic priorities. Pima also aligned its organizational, financial, and data resources to support its workforce mission to "improve the responsiveness and programs of Pima Community College to meet the needs of the business community and economic development opportunities."[16]

Transforming Pima's Organizational Structure

CONSOLIDATED REPORTING LINES

Pima consolidated reporting lines to make it easier for employers to navigate Pima's workforce development offerings. In 2013, Pima had six campuses, each operating independently with its own president, deans, and support services.[17] College stakeholders highlighted that this organizational structure confused employers and resulted in duplication at Pima. Thus, Pima transitioned from six campus presidents to one and centralized essential support services such as finance and IT.

> "Workforce development is a paradigm that Pima applies across the institution, not a siloed program or a department."
> —Dr. Ian Roark, Vice President of Workforce Development and Strategic Partnerships at Pima

Today, the chancellor has seven direct vice chancellor reports, including the president and executive vice chancellor (EVC) for student experience and workforce.[18] In conversation, Lambert called out that the purpose of including workforce within the scope of the EVC role was to cement workforce development as a top institutional priority. The president and EVC oversees the entire workforce development division and is responsible for integrating a workforce development focus throughout the college.

ONE-STOP SHOP FOR INDUSTRY

Pima established a one-stop shop for industry engagement to make it easier for employers to find education and training solutions. College stakeholders mentioned that Pima lacked a comprehensive workforce development division in 2013. As a result, employers had to navigate through multiple campuses and departments to find the right college partners for their needs. To address employers' frustration, Lambert established a vice president (VP) of workforce development—later designated as the VP of workforce development and strategic partnerships.

The VP of workforce and strategic partnerships is the single point of contact for any employer, industry, and/or economic development engagement at Pima. The VP oversees the workforce development division and reports directly to the president and EVC for student experience and workforce. Any new workforce development initiatives are incubated through the workforce development division. Economic development organizations and employers highlighted that the creation of this position sent a signal to employers about Pima's commitment to workforce development and addressing employer pain points.

> "This [organizational transformation] was an acknowledgement that workforce was going to be part of Pima's portfolio, and it was a signal to external partners that workforce was not limited to just noncredit contract training."
> —Dr. Aaron Ball, Director of College and Career Pathways at the Center for the Future of Arizona

MATRIXED REPORTING

Pima implemented a matrixed reporting structure for the workforce development division, which enabled Pima to better integrate workforce development throughout the college. Roark explained that the division operates as a horizontal, rather than vertical, function. Every dean who reports to the provost also has a dotted reporting line to the president and EVC for student experience and workforce and the VP of workforce development and strategic partnerships. This matrixed reporting structure makes it easier for the workforce development division to support faculty and staff across the college and apply a workforce development lens to every education and training program.

A COMPREHENSIVE AND EMPOWERED WORKFORCE DEVELOPMENT DIVISION

Pima expanded the scope of its workforce development division to better serve the diverse needs of its employers and learners. In 2013, the existing workforce development division contained continuing education, Pima for Youth (K–12 camps), and a business engagement team that was primarily focused on contract training. As per interviews with college stakeholders, Pima expanded the workforce development division's purview to include credit and noncredit industry partnership programs, tuition assistance, and work-based learning (e.g., internships, apprenticeships, job shadows).

To facilitate this change, Pima removed the division's balanced budget requirement. College stakeholders explained that the division was historically required to generate the revenue it needed to cover the entirety of its expenses. As a result, the division prioritized high-revenue noncredit programs and didn't have an incentive to collaborate with academic departments to design other programs for employers. Once Pima removed the balanced budget requirement and started funding the division out of the general fund, the division started to collaborate with other departments and expand its portfolio of offerings for industry.

Pima has since continued to expand the workforce development division. The division now houses five teams—the Business Engagement Team, Small Business Development Center, Employer Engagement and Career Services, Emerging Innovation, and Community and Corporate Navigation of Lifelong Learning—and three programs: Public Safety and Security, Center for

Transportation Training, and Prison Program. Denise Kingman, Pima's director of employer engagement and career services, explained that Pima made a deliberate decision to move career services into the workforce development division to ensure that employers and learners had a one-stop shop for talent development and hiring. Pima also decided to locate the Emerging Innovation team within the division as the division had historically been the college's innovation incubator.

Resource Alignment to Support Pima's Workforce Mission

Even before the COVID-19 pandemic exacerbated financial pressures facing postsecondary institutions, Pima had needed to adapt to a challenging funding environment in Arizona. Arizona state funding for community colleges decreased significantly between 2009 and 2016. Over this period, Pima's state funding fell from approximately $1,000 to $0 per full-time student equivalent and from $3.25 million to $0 for capital outlays.[19] This reduction in state funding represented a 12 percent decrease in Pima's total budget.[20] Adding to financial pressures, Pima's enrollments declined over the same period: full-time student equivalents dropped from just over 20,000 to 14,429.[21]

College stakeholders recall that Pima did not expect state funding to rebound. Therefore, Pima made difficult cost-cutting decisions—selling campuses, eliminating positions, and sunsetting low-enrollment programs. Although these actions were necessary given the funding environment, Chancellor Lambert viewed the situation as an opportunity to refocus investment toward Pima's strategic priorities and grow revenues from alternative sources, including industry. Employers not only had the demand for talent but the budgets to pay for programs to upskill and reskill their existing workforces and invest in joint facilities and equipment. By better aligning its offerings with industry, Pima could offset the revenue declines due to state funding reductions and decreasing enrollments and stabilize future revenue generation.

Over the last decade, Pima aligned its resources to support its workforce mission. Historically, the majority of Pima's revenue was generated by property taxes, followed by grants, tuition, philanthropy, and contracts. According to Lambert, Pima prioritized growing its property tax, industry, and philanthropic revenues.[22] In parallel, Pima underwent a large reorganization and cost-cutting effort. During this time, Pima redirected resources to career and technical education and addressed financial disincentives to collaboration such as the workforce development division's balanced budget requirement.[23]

As Pima's property tax revenues grew, Pima was still subject to an expenditure limit on the amount of tax revenue it could spend annually per Arizona state law. In November 2020, the public approved Proposition 481, which raised the expenditure limit, giving Pima the flexibility to spend its collected tax revenue on its education programs.[24]

As a result of these financial realignments, Pima has been able to seed innovative workforce development funds, according to Lambert. For example, Pima created a $1 million innovation seed fund and an industry training fund. These funds further help incentivize workforce development innovations in response to labor market needs.

Embracing a Data-Driven Mindset

Pima recognized that data was integral to ensure its programs provided pathways to high-demand jobs and made data a top institutional priority. For instance, the chancellor highlighted the importance of data by creating a chief strategist and assistant vice chancellor of strategy, analytics, and research position on his leadership team and promoting Pima's head of institutional research into the role. College stakeholders mentioned that Pima became more data-focused and data-driven in making decisions because of this change.

In addition, Pima invested $500,000 to build its data warehouse and improve its business intelligence system, according to Dr. Nicola Richmond, Pima's chief strategist. Pima hired a third-party consultant to drive the effort. Pima also deliberately invested in a noncredit registration system, including integration with Pima's data warehouse so that all learner data could be accessed in one place. Today, Pima's student information system collects rich data on its credit and noncredit learners, including enrollment, completion, retention, wages, and survey data about learners and faculty.[25] The new business intelligence system provides real-time data to Pima's leadership, faculty, and staff through interactive and custom reporting.

Pima uses its data to inform key strategic, operational, and programmatic decisions. College stakeholders highlighted how Pima uses local market data from Emsi Burning Glass, a firm that specializes in labor market data, to assess regional occupation gaps and salary growth. The strategy, research, and analytics team then provides this data to the workforce development division, which uses it to inform regional economic development conversations and new program and curriculum development. Further, Pima uses its extensive learner demographic, retention, and completion data to inform learner support initiatives.

Pima continues to enhance its data capabilities. Dr. Richmond mentioned that Pima is currently expanding data collection on alumni and noncredit learners. As part of this effort, Pima is working with the State of Arizona to establish a longitudinal database to better understand how graduates progress in the workforce.

Adapting to the COVID-19 Pandemic Aftermath

In the 1940s, Pima County witnessed fast population growth due to activities at Davis-Monthan Air Force Base and WWII.[26] Pima County's population continued to grow through the turn of the century, with companies in aerospace and defense, manufacturing, mining, and education employing many residents. The 2007–2009 Great Recession hit Pima County particularly hard.[27] Before the recession, Tucson's job growth rates were among the highest in the US, but they were concentrated in the services and construction sectors. These sectors were disproportionately affected during the recession, and Pima County recovered slowly.[28] Between 2010 and 2019, in Arizona and the US, total employment grew by approximately 23 percent[29] and 16 percent,[30] respectively, while in Pima County, total employment grew by only 10 percent.[31] In 2020, the pandemic introduced labor market uncertainty, and Pima saw a drop in employment of approximately 4 percent[32]—compared to the statewide decline of 3 percent.[33]

On the heels of the pandemic, and more than a decade after the Great Recession, Pima County is focusing on recovery and driving economic growth through business retention, expansion, and attraction in priority industries.[34] The county sees Pima as a key partner in driving this workforce development agenda.[35] Pima County's latest economic development plan highlights how the county will rely on Pima to support this effort: "Pima County's strategy must focus on training the existing workforce for higher-skilled jobs in strategic industry sectors . . . Pima County One-Stop will work collaboratively with Pima Community College (PCC) and other providers to . . . be more

> "Pima sees its role in the community as a driver of, rather than a reactor to, the economy."
>
> —Joe Snell,
> President and CEO
> of Sun Corridor Inc.

predictive in developing and implementing technical education programming that is aligned to business and industry needs."[36]

In the aftermath of the COVID-19 pandemic, Pima is well-positioned to support the county in achieving its goals. Based on employment forecasts, technician-level occupations in fields ranging from aviation to healthcare are among the most in demand in Pima County.[37] Pima offers strong technician training in medicine and health and applied tech fields such as auto, aviation, building and construction, machining and welding, and mining.[38] Pima has also expanded stackable credentials.[39]

Over the last decade, Pima has turned around its relationships with employers and cemented itself as a driver of workforce development in the region. Pima is continuously improving and innovating ways to meet the needs of its learners and the community, even in the wake of the pandemic. The next section will highlight Pima's successful efforts to establish innovative industry partnerships, create flexible career pathways, and offer work-based learning, all while supporting learners to succeed.

PIMA TODAY

Innovative Industry Partnerships

Pima has been able to satisfy regional employers and prepare its learners for in-demand jobs through its diverse employer partnerships. Pima is the only community college for a region with twenty thousand employer establishments, and it represents an important talent pipeline and training center.[40] Pima partners with employers on topics ranging from economic development to program curricula. Pima has been able to build deep relationships with employers through numerous efforts, including board leadership, industry advisory committees, and especially its centers of excellence (COEs).

Pima has also become a major player in the region's economic development strategy.

David Welsh, executive vice president of Sun Corridor Inc., Tucson's regional economic development entity, says, "Working with Lee and Ian and their team is night-and-day different than working with their predecessors. They are an integral part of our team. They're constantly working with us to offer up the best we can to prospective industries. They truly understand that their work has to be demand-driven: they are great partners."

CENTERS OF EXCELLENCE

Pima developed its COEs to enable the college to better anticipate and respond to labor market needs in primary sectors of the economy. Each COE is aligned to a specific sector and provides learners with multiple on-ramps to degrees, certificates, and training. The centers offer cutting-edge equipment and facilities for experiential learning that augment online, hybrid, and in-person lessons. In addition, the COEs provide a structure to bring employer, community, and educational partners together to share sector-relevant expertise, develop curricular best practices, and provide thought leadership on workforce development.[41]

According to interviews with college stakeholders, the workforce development division and faculty started developing the idea for the COEs in 2017. They spearheaded a series of industry summits, attended by over 120 employers, to gain input. Pima hired an external facilitator to facilitate the summits and later replicated summit discussions with learners, community partners, faculty, and staff to understand how to best design the centers. Throughout the design process, Pima conducted market analysis to refine the sectors, benchmarked programs, and maintained ongoing dialogue with key stakeholders. Pima's board supported the COEs and approved $65 million in funding from revenue bonds to seed the effort, according to Chancellor Lambert.

Pima's first COE, in applied technology, opened in 2021 in a fifty-thousand-square-foot facility. The center is home to the Automotive Technology and Innovation Center, the Advanced Manufacturing Building, and the Aviation Technology Center. The Automotive Technology and Innovation Center features programs in diesel, electric, and autonomous vehicles. The Advanced Manufacturing Building houses programs in automated industrial tech, computer-aided design, machining, and welding. The Aviation Technology Center is located in hangar space at Tucson International Airport and is expected to double the number of learners

"Pima is distinctive in that its leadership goes above and beyond to engage and establish relationships with local industry leaders like myself. It then relies on those relationships to help build and improve on curriculum, and at the same time help to get its students a foot in the door with these industries."

—Calline Sanchez, Vice President, IBM

enrolled in Pima's aviation repair and maintenance program. The COE houses numerous programs in partnership with industry, such as the Applied Technology Academy (see the Applied Technology Academy box ahead).[42]

Pima has five additional COEs aligned to key sectors:[43]

- The Center of Excellence in Health Professions, which provides training in numerous healthcare programs such as nursing, surgical technology, and medical lab technology and supports multiple pathways to healthcare professions. Pima will be developing a space that resembles a hospital environment to improve the learning experience.

Applied Technology Academy

The Applied Technology Academy, housed in the COE in Applied Technology, is an innovative partnership between Pima and Caterpillar. According to interviews with college stakeholders, Caterpillar had identified that its engineers lacked factory-floor fabrication experience, resulting in designs that were difficult to implement on the factory floor. The workforce development division convened Pima's applied technology faculty and Caterpillar engineers to dive into the issue and design a training solution, now known as the Applied Technology Academy. In the academy, Caterpillar engineers take six-week lab-based classes to get real-world experience in machining and welding. The academy is a noncredit program, supported by investment from Caterpillar. According to college leaders, Caterpillar showcased the academy to Arizona's governor, which later catalyzed the state's $15 million investment in the Aviation Technology Center.

"We came to Pima Community College with a vision to develop our employees and further enhance Caterpillar's world class design capability through the manufacturing trades," said Jean Savage, Vice President for Caterpillar's Surface Mining & Technology Division. "The team at Pima shared our passion for continual learning and for building technical talent in the local community through innovative partnerships like this . . . The benefits of Applied Technology Academy are tremendous, and we're proud to be part of it."[44]

- The Center of Excellence in Information Technology and Cybersecurity, which offers the only "live-fire" cyber range at a community college. The center offers learners hands-on experiences through the live-fire environment, a student-run data center, and a cybersecurity operations center.
- The Center of Excellence in Public Safety and Security, which houses Fire Science and Emergency Medical Services and the Law Enforcement Academy and Administration of Justice.
- The Center of Excellence in Hospitality and Tourism, which will be open to the public and home to multiple commercial kitchens, a restaurant, a grill, and hotel suite learning labs. Pima will be funding the space through a $2.7 million Title V grant.
- The Center of Excellence in Arts and Humanities, which features performance space and art galleries so that learners can have experiential learning opportunities.

LEADERSHIP ON REGIONAL BOARDS

Pima's participation on numerous boards demonstrates how significantly Pima has revitalized its relationships with employers. According to interviews with college and economic development stakeholders, Pima's leadership and faculty are active members of boards and councils, including employer boards, regional workforce boards, and industry cluster boards. As a result, Pima is well-positioned to shape the economic development agenda of the region and develop programs and curriculum in anticipation of employer demand.

Due to these deep relationships, Pima also works with employer and economic development partners to advocate for career-focused education for community colleges in Arizona broadly. College stakeholders highlighted how Pima has worked with partners to shape and advocate for two pieces of legislation—one to expand dual enrollment and one to allow community colleges to offer baccalaureate degrees—both of which passed. According to James Palacios, Pima's director of dual enrollment and high school programs, "Pima Community College believes in strong partnership through collaboration and creates innovative opportunities for positive change in our secondary schools; Pima is working hard to break down barriers our community high schools and students face."

INDUSTRY ADVISORY COMMITTEES

At Pima's industry advisory committees, faculty and industry share and discuss industry trends, new technology and equipment, and curricula to ensure that Pima's programs are well-aligned with employer needs. Historically, however, Pima's advisory committees were not well-attended by industry partners or well-regarded by faculty. According to interviews with college stakeholders, some faculty treated the committees as something they had to do to "check the box," rather than an opportunity to discuss meaningful program feedback with industry partners.

Pima sought to change the culture and improve the quality of Pima's industry advisory committees. As was mentioned in college stakeholder interviews, Pima hired a third-party consultant to help identify opportunities for improvement. The consultant interviewed committee members, facilitated meetings, and worked with the workforce development division to establish improved procedures and standards. In some program divisions, Pima consolidated its industry and high school advisory committees into one, resulting in better attended and more cohesive committee meetings. Now, Pima's industry advisory committees are effective mechanisms for dialogue with industry, which helps Pima ensure that programs satisfy labor market demands.

Flexible Career Pathways

Pima is distinctive in its ability to create flexible *pathways*, combinations of education and training that prepare individuals to enter or advance in occupations that are aligned with the skill needs of the regional economy. Pima offers a full spectrum of education and training programs, including career-focused high school and adult basic education programs, micropathways, certificates, and degrees. Learners can choose from fully online, hybrid, or in-person programs. These offerings provide new majority learners with opportunities to earn stackable credentials while meeting the talent requirements of employers.

DUAL ENROLLMENT AND HIGH SCHOOL PROGRAMS

Pima's dual enrollment program allows high school students to take courses and earn college credit that they can apply toward a certificate or degree in the future. Over the last ten years, Pima has expanded its dual enrollment program to "inspire and inform high school students and their families about education and career connected pathways that are focused on preparing students for success in high-demand, high-wage STEM professions."[45] Pima's dual enrollment courses are offered in online, hybrid, or in-person formats to provide flexibility for high school partners.

In 2019, Pima hired a new director of dual enrollment and high school programs, James Palacios, to expand the program. During the director's tenure, dual enrollment learner headcount grew from 2,290 in 2019 to 4,600 in 2022, while the number of Pima's high school partners doubled.[46] To drive growth, the director concentrated on maintaining and repairing old high school relationships and establishing new high school partnerships. Pima worked closely with high school partners to reduce barriers to application and enrollment. Pima was also involved in advocating for the removal of a statewide limitation on the number of high school freshmen and sophomores who can participate in dual enrollment.

In addition to dual enrollment, Pima is exploring ways to expose high school learners to different education and career pathways. In interviews, college stakeholders highlight that Pima hired high school transition coaches to help high school students navigate postsecondary pathways. Pima also oversees Pima for Youth, noncredit bootcamps intended to facilitate career exploration and connection to dual enrollment opportunities for K–12 learners. Pima is currently experimenting with introducing apprenticeship-style opportunities to this program.

ADULT BASIC EDUCATION FOR COLLEGE AND CAREER

At Pima, the saying "a learner is a learner is a learner" is used commonly. Pima strives to blur the lines between credit and noncredit learners, and this philosophy extends to Pima's Adult Basic Education for College and Career (ABECC) programs. ABECC is seen as a vital part of Pima's workforce ecosystem. In fact, Amanda Abens, dean of workforce development and continuing education, mentioned that Pima deliberately changed the name of Adult Basic Education to Adult Basic Education for College and Career to demonstrate its commitment to college and career for all learners.

Learners enrolled in Pima's ABECC learn a workforce-relevant curriculum and receive career exploration support. Laurie Kierstead-Joseph, assistant vice chancellor for ABECC, highlighted ABECC's Integrated Basic Education and

Skills Training (IBEST) as a flagship program. IBEST is a national instruction model that allows learners to work toward their GEDs and obtain certificates in career or technical fields. IBEST integrates career education into the curriculum and is taught jointly by technical and nontechnical faculty. Pima opened its IBEST programs to both learners who were working toward their GEDs and those who had already earned their GEDs once Pima realized both sets of learners could benefit. GED and non-GED seekers now enroll in and take IBEST classes side by side.

ABECC works closely with the workforce development division and other partners to assess labor market data to determine which IBEST programs to offer. Further, the Office of Workforce and Strategic Partnerships advocates for these programs and educates employer partners about how IBEST and other ABECC programs can provide them with a pipeline of talent.

Pima's IBEST programs have been successful: approximately 75 percent of IBEST learners go on to complete their college certificates and 81 percent find employment within twelve months of finishing their IBEST programs.[47] Pima remains committed to continuously improving its IBEST programs through investment in professional learning and development.

PIMA FAST TRACK

The COVID-19 pandemic intensified the need for more flexible educational offerings to address underemployment and unemployment in Arizona.[48] In response, Pima developed fast track programs to prepare workers to meet employer demand in key regional industries. These programs are *micropathways*, defined as two or more stackable credentials that allow learners to upgrade their skills quickly and that can lead to a job in a high-demand occupation.

Pima received $100,000 from the Education Design Lab to develop a minimum of three micropathways to enroll at least six hundred learners.[49] Over fifteen months, Pima identified and created eight micropathway programs, including Electrical, Carpentry, Information Technology, and Emergency Medical Services. According to interviews with college stakeholders, Pima identified high-demand and high-mobility occupations, informed by labor market data from Emsi Burning Glass, and worked with deans and employers to determine skills required to fill those occupations. By the end of the design process, Pima had engaged over sixty stakeholders, including

deans, faculty, employers, and learners, on program curricula and structure.

Pima launched its first micropathway cohorts in the fall of 2021. Pima's micropathways
are competency-based, multimodal, and stackable.[50] Each micropathway is based on compe-
tency frameworks and is available in an online,
hybrid, or in-person format to provide learners
with maximum flexibility. Upon completion,
learners can earn employer-recognized credentials and stack their micropathways into future
certificates or degrees to further advance in their chosen career fields.[51]

> "The pandemic has brought a heightened sense of urgency to our historic mission of supporting social and economic mobility for the diverse students and working adults that community colleges serve. Addressing this crisis requires us to develop new and more flexible credentials that are more responsive to the rapidly changing needs of the labor market."
>
> —*Lee Lambert, Chancellor of Pima Community College*[52]

PRIOR LEARNING ASSESSMENT

Pima's ability to provide flexible pathways and stackable credentials is enabled
by its strong prior learning assessment (PLA) regimen. PLA is a process that
colleges use to award learners with credit for knowledge that they have ac-
quired from previous personal and/or professional experiences. One-third of
Pima's for-credit courses can be earned through PLA from one or more of
the following categories: noncredit, industry-recognized credential, challenge
exam, portfolio, or military experience and training.[53] Learners can earn up to
75 percent of the credits needed for a degree or certificate through PLA.[54] PLA
is lower than the cost of tuition, so learners can earn their credentials faster
while also saving money.[55]

According to interviews, the workforce development division first concep-
tualized and operationalized PLA at Pima. With the support of the chancellor,
the division worked with faculty to identify opportunities to implement PLA.
As more faculty saw the benefit of PLA, the number of courses eligible for
PLA grew. Although one-third of Pima's credit courses can be earned through
PLA today, Pima is continuing to work with faculty to expand PLA across all
departments.

Work-Based Learning for All

Pima is committed to ensuring that 100 percent of its learners have a work-
based learning experience. Work-based learning is an approach that provides

learners with formal and informal real-life work experiences, online or in-person. Work-based learning can help learners improve their job readiness while satisfying the talent needs of employers.[56] Pima's Employer Engagement and Career Services team helps learners access work-based learning and full-time employment opportunities. At Pima, work-based learning encompasses anything from microinternships and job shadowing to internships and apprenticeships.[57] Both credit and noncredit learners are eligible to participate in work-based learning opportunities.

Pima continues to innovate its work-based learning opportunities. According to Denise Kingman, director of Employer Engagement and Career Services, the team is baselining each department to assess opportunities to establish and expand work-based learning so that 100 percent of learners can have a work-based learning experience. Further, the team is hiring career navigators, who will be aligned to Pima's COE sectors, to help learners pursue work-based learning and full-time opportunities.

Learner Supports

Pima's commitment to supporting learners has enabled it to be a successful, workforce-focused community college. An overwhelming percentage of Pima's enrolled learners work, and 36 percent of Pima's learners come from the bottom 40 percent of the US income distribution.[58] Most learners are part-time and thus not always eligible for financial aid. Therefore, Pima invests in offering holistic support to new majority learners.

According to interviews with college stakeholders, Pima leverages government grants to address barriers to learning such as food insecurity and childcare. Pima further reduces financial barriers through braided funding and initiatives such as Earn to Learn, free open educational resources (OERs), twenty-nine-day billing and grade reporting, and PLA:[59]

- *Earn to Learn:* Earn to Learn is a matched savings scholarship program and is often considered a supplement to the federal Pell Grant program. Multiple institutions in Arizona have partnered with Earn to Learn to provide learners with scholarships, coaching, and financial education.

- *Free open educational resources:* Pima has pursued a large OER initiative to drive down textbook costs since the 2016–2017 academic year. OERs are freely accessible instructional materials (text, media, etc.). Pima is planning to expand OERs to more courses.
- *Twenty-nine-day billing and grade reporting:* Pima committed to provide bills and grades within twenty-nine days of exams to reduce barriers to reenrollment for learners receiving tuition reimbursement from employers. Most employers wait for grades to determine tuition reimbursement. If grading and billing timelines are not in sync, learners can face financial uncertainty about the level of reimbursement, and this can deter reenrollment. Thus, Pima worked with employers to sync billing and grade reporting timelines.
- *Prior learning assessment:* One-third of Pima's credit classes are eligible for credit through PLA, and up to 75 percent of a certificate or degree can be earned through PLA. As a result, learners do not have to pay for courses with content they already know.[60]

CONCLUSION

The Pima story exemplifies what a community college can accomplish when its top leaders make workforce development a strategic priority and focus organizational, financial, and data resources on supporting the economic advancement goals of its learners. From launching centers of excellence to flexible micropathways, Pima continues to innovate ways to put learners on paths to economic and social mobility.

Pima's journey doesn't end here. The road to recovery from the COVID-19 pandemic offers both challenges and opportunities. The pandemic intensified labor market uncertainty and accelerated declines in enrollment: Pima saw over an eight-thousand-person decline in enrollment in credit and noncredit courses between 2019 and 2021. However, as adult learners are looking for opportunities to reskill, Pima is well-positioned to respond.[61] Pima already offers a breadth of short-term and long-term career pathways to in-demand jobs and works closely with employers to align

> "Pima meets the learner where they are and gives them what they need to be successful."
> —Amanda Abens, Dean of Workforce Development and Continuing Education, Pima Community College

educational programs with changing labor market needs. The college is also experienced in providing working learners the flexibility and support they need to succeed. While the road may be long, Pima has a critical role to play in connecting education and employment and driving inclusive economic recovery and growth in the region.

CHAPTER 5

Power of Active Listening

San Jacinto Community College's Key to
Meaningful Employer Partnerships

Sakshee Chawla

EXECUTIVE SUMMARY

Home to the Houston Ship Channel, NASA's Johnson Space Center, and over four hundred chemical plants, East Harris County represents a diverse, expanding Texas economy. San Jacinto College (a.k.a. San Jac) sits at the very center of this ecosystem. As a majority-minority community college serving over 41,500 students, San Jac provides the critical connection point between the region's growing population and high-demand jobs in maritime, petrochemical, aerospace, healthcare, IT, and supply chain management. Today, San Jac embodies a model for how to make an educational system responsive to a region's economic needs.

San Jac is known across the region for its ability to build strategic partnerships with employers, intermediary organizations, and government institutions. In fact, many local actors cite this external orientation as the college's biggest strength. San Jac aims to embed employer input and feedback at every stage of program development and improvement. The college's commitment to listening to industry and soliciting proactive employer participation takes multiple forms.

San Jac has established itself as a leading player in Greater Houston's economic development strategy. The college created a new entity called the Chancellor's Advisory Council, cochaired by regional C-suite leaders and San Jac's chancellor. In addition, the college is represented on the boards of essentially all major economic initiatives in the region—including the Economic Alliance Houston Port Region, Bay Area Houston Economic Partnership, East Harris County Manufacturers Association, Greater Houston Partnership's UpSkill Houston, Aspen Institute's Communities that Work Partnership, and Texas Talent Pipeline Management (TPM). This means that rarely does a conversation about the region's labor needs take place without San Jac playing a major role at the table.

This approach is only possible because the college has successfully integrated the economic mission of the region into its own human capital strategy. Executive leaders, faculty, and staff at San Jac are all evaluated on their ability to embrace the college's commitment to its student success and workforce mission. As part of their personal key performance indicators (KPIs), college employees are assessed on the number and quality of partnerships they establish. In addition, the college recruits senior leaders from emerging local industries to bring the credibility and expertise needed to build and scale new programs.

To support students' economic mobility goals, San Jac integrates intensive career exploration and career advising into its approach for all students. From the very start of the student journey at San Jac, students begin the discussion of career choices and pathways. They participate in discussions of career exploration with an advisor or faculty member in orientation and during a first-semester course designed to introduce career and college exploration and planning. The college also aligned the rollout of its academic program redesign (*guided pathways*) to better map high school coursework and college "metamajors" to career pathways. By 2021, San Jac had reduced the share of general studies awards by almost half in just five years.

Finally, San Jac has effectively utilized investments in non-credit-bearing programs as incubators for new programs in growing fields. The process of creating new for-credit offerings can take years. San Jac leadership has embraced noncredit programs as an entrepreneurial strategy to respond to new demands more quickly in the labor market and integrate employer feedback on program design much closer to real time. This model allows the college to continue to refine the program after launch. In addition, the different revenue model for noncredit courses helps prove that the program is truly in demand from employers and students. After securing an initial investment and partners, the college works to quickly transition the program so that students can receive academic credit. San Jac has successfully employed this strategy for fields ranging from maritime to aerospace.

INTRODUCTION

Located in the Greater Houston area, San Jacinto College is a minority-majority community college serving more than forty thousand students across five campuses.[1] Surrounded by the Houston Ship Channel, petrochemical

TABLE 5.1 San Jacinto Community College quick facts*

Location	Houston-The Woodlands-Sugar Land, TX (Suburban, South)
Percentage of county residents who hold a bachelor's degree or above	32.3%
Median household income of county residents	$63,022
Total unduplicated enrollment count of credit and noncredit students	44,947
Percentage credit vs. noncredit	91% credit/9% noncredit
Percentage of full-time vs. part-time students (credit students only)	6% full-time/94% part-time
Percentage of students who received Pell Grants (credit students only)	40%
Percentage of students from the bottom 40% of the income distribution (credit students only)	34%

Sources: College Scorecard, 2021; US Department of Commerce Economics and Statistics Administration, US Census Bureau, US Department of Housing and Urban Development; US. Census Bureau, 2020; San Jacinto Community College; Raj Chetty, John Friedman, Emmanuel Saez, Nicholas Turner, and Danny Yagan, Mobility Report Cards: The Role of Colleges in Intergenerational Mobility, NBER Working Paper No. 23618, 2017.

*Enrollment data represents 2021–2022 numbers, inclusive of credit, noncredit, and dual enrollment students, as provided by San Jacinto Community College.

FIGURE 5.1 San Jac enrollment by race/ethnicity, 2021–2022 academic year

FIGURE 5.2 San Jac enrollment by gender, 2021–2022 academic year

FIGURE 5.3 San Jac students by enrollment type (credit only), 2021–2022 academic year

FIGURE 5.4 San Jac enrollment by age, 2021–2022 academic year

industry, and the Johnson Space Center, San Jac has emerged as the college and training partner of choice for East Harris County, Texas. By offering robust workforce credentials and prebaccalaureate associate's degrees, it trains students for jobs in industries including maritime, petrochemical, aerospace, and healthcare.[2] San Jac's contribution to the regional economy is estimated to be around $1.3 billion, supporting more than 13,044 jobs.[3] It estimates that for every dollar a student invests in their education at San Jac, they see a $6.30 return in future income.[4]

Historically, Houston's economy was primarily known for its production of oil and gas.[5] Today, Houston is also a world leader in the chemical industry and is home to 405 chemical plants that employ nearly thirty-six thousand people.[6] Houston has also played an important role in space exploration with NASA's Johnson Space Center as the focal point of the US manned space flight program.[7] The transportation and logistics, healthcare, construction, and biomedical research industries also represent industry clusters in the region.[8] The shifting industry clusters have influenced workforce needs in Houston and pushed community colleges like San Jac to offer academic programs that prepare students for employment in the economy.

San Jacinto's role as a regional workforce development and training leader is a result of its market-responsive and strategic partnerships with employers, educational organizations, and government institutions within and beyond the Greater Houston area. In particular, it has attracted more than $41 million in workforce-related grants since 2012 to train Houston workers by serving on boards and committees, including chambers of commerce, economic development councils, city and county governments, and nonprofits.[9] Through partnerships with industry leaders, San Jac built its Maritime Technology and Training Center, the LyondellBasell Center for Petrochemical, Energy, and Technology, and the EDGE Center at the Houston Spaceport. Students use cutting-edge equipment and technology to gain hands-on, practical skills while also interacting with employers through resume workshops and networking opportunities.

Since 2009, San Jac has awarded nearly fifty-four thousand degrees and certifications, including thirteen thousand trade certifications.[10] In addition to increasing enrollment by 20 percent, it also increased its three-year graduation and transfer rate from 29 percent to 38 percent in the past five years.[11]

"This is a remarkable time to be at San Jacinto College. We're producing more career opportunities for our graduates than ever before, through partnerships with global leaders in government, business, and healthcare. We're aggressively improving our training programs in science, technology, engineering, and math to fill national job shortages and get students excited about STEM careers. And we're making college more viable with strategies such as our Achieving the Dream initiative," said Chancellor Brenda Hellyer.[12]

The Aspen Institute recognized San Jac's work across teaching and learning, degree completion and transfer to four-year institutions, success in the workforce, and equitable outcomes for diverse student groups. After being selected as a Rising Star Award recipient in 2017 and a Top 10 Community College in 2019, San Jac was designated a Finalist with Distinction out of more than 1,100 community colleges across the country in 2021.[13] San Jac has also received the Achieving the Dream Leader College hallmark and Achieving the Dream Leader College of Distinction status for its strong student outcomes and narrowing equity gaps.[14]

The onset of the COVID-19 pandemic forced San Jac to quickly pivot in-person classes to online programming that students could complete from their homes. Leaders at San Jac suggest that the college was uniquely positioned to adapt quickly because of its experience managing instructional continuity and recovery after Hurricanes Ike and Harvey. The college's decision to continue to hold in-person classes was appreciated by regional employers who valued hands-on learning experiences to train future employees. Although enrollment declined slightly during the pandemic, the college's decision to remain open throughout the pandemic likely prevented a more significant decline in enrollment. In particular, the college reported enrolling approximately 31,500 students in fall 2020 and 31,100 students in fall 2021.[15] These enrollment numbers were only slightly lower than the enrollments of 32,000 and 32,500 students in fall 2018 and fall 2019, respectively.[16]

LISTENING TO INDUSTRY

Partnership with employers and key industry leaders is critical to San Jac's workforce development mission. San Jac stays responsive to local workforce needs by partnering with key industries in the region, developing training centers in collaboration with local employers, and establishing degrees and credentials in high-demand fields.[17]

These partnerships are important to ensure that San Jac is designing and offering academic programs that prepare graduates for workforce demands. Employer partnerships are also necessary to build new academic buildings and facilities or gain access to new equipment. Updates to infrastructure and machinery allow for improvements to faculty teaching and student learning while also enabling the college to meet regional workforce demands. Employer partnerships have enabled the college to increase the courses and programs it offers, contributing to an increase in the number of graduates in areas including maritime, pipefitting and welding, construction, manufacturing, and healthcare to fill the skills gap in the region.

> "San Jacinto College is proactive. The college is there, engaged with the community, engaged with the city, engaged with the industry trying to solve the problem."
>
> —Steve Altemus,
> President and CEO
> of Intuitive Machines

Most community colleges understand the importance of employer partners in designing and developing a new workforce program but rarely act on it effectively. San Jac's ability to actively listen to employers and adapt in response to feedback is what differentiates its approach to workforce development. When San Jac first began to develop its maritime program, feedback from regional employers and industry leaders enabled the college to make informed decisions about where to build the maritime campus and how to structure the building. San Jac was originally planning to build its maritime campus inland but adjusted its plans in order to build the campus on water after alarms from industry partners. Without the crucial feedback from employers, San Jac would have lost credibility, which would also lead to its training not being utilized by industry.

Lessons from this experience made the college leadership team recognize that "industry is the true expert" and needs to be trusted to guide key programmatic decisions. Following this experience, San Jac focused on developing employer participation early during the development and launch of the petrochemical and aerospace programs. Meetings with industry leaders resulted in San Jac rethinking elements of the program, including the size of classrooms, equipment needed, and alignment of curriculum. San Jac held forums, collected employer feedback on curriculum design, identified potential faculty and teachers in its programs, and developed labs in partnership with local companies. Today, the college has employers present in its academic buildings, interacting with students, and conducting interviews on-site, which helps demonstrate their interest in and commitment to hiring students from the college.

Input and feedback from employers are not limited to technical curricula design but extend to soft skill training as well. For example, faculty and instructors identified opportunities to integrate soft skills, including management, teamwork, and basic safety skills, once employers identified these skills as lacking among San Jac graduates.

When San Jac received employer feedback that its petrochemical program's curriculum and equipment were not aligned with new improvements in the field, the college added more hands-on instruction, improved its facilities, and hired instructors trained in the new technology. This responsiveness to feedback was rewarded when the college secured significant industry involvement

> "Our approach with employers is to learn the good, the bad, and the ugly. Of course, we want to know what we are doing effectively. But more importantly, we want to know what we are not doing effectively and identify areas where our employer partners would recommend we focus our efforts."
>
> —*Allatia Harris, Vice Chancellor for Strategic Initiatives, Workforce Development, Community Relations, and Diversity*

in curriculum development, financial investment in facilities and equipment, and employee engagement with students, resulting in a commitment that employers would hire qualified San Jac grads after changes were implemented. Its strategic relationships with employers and responsiveness to workforce needs have yielded strong results for students. In particular, graduates from the associate of applied science degree at San Jac earned nearly $15,000 more than the average new hire in the county.[18]

Chancellor's Advisory Council

The focus on workforce development begins with Hellyer and her executive leadership team, but is emphasized throughout the organizational structure, regardless of tenure and function. Most community colleges have program advisory committees, but San Jac's Chancellor's Advisory Council seems to be uniquely impactful. Although Texas requires all colleges to use program advisory committees to inform workforce development efforts, these committees typically comprise less tenured staff and rarely include representation from executive leaders. In comparison, each Chancellor's Advisory Council at San Jac is cochaired by the chancellor and a leader from the industry and includes C-suite leaders recruited from regional employers. Faculty and other representatives from San Jac may also attend meetings and participate in conversations about workforce development. Industry leaders, in addition to representatives from San Jac, design and set the agenda for these meetings.

During Chancellor's Advisory Council meetings, leaders from the relevant industry discuss challenges in the hiring environment, identify new technical developments, and offer feedback on new program development or continuous program improvement. Chancellor's Advisory Council meetings are used by San Jac to discuss academic programs, receive feedback from employers, and identify areas for improvement. Representation from executive leaders in the regional economy enables San Jac to learn about changes in employer demand and access strategic information that is not discussed by traditional program advisory committees.

Program Advisory Committees

The Chancellor's Advisory Council also helps San Jac identify potential representatives for the program advisory committees. Because C-suite leaders often recommend employees to the program advisory committees, access to the C-suite leaders through the Chancellor's Advisory Council improves attendance, participation, and interactions in the program advisory committees. A step below the Chancellor's Advisory Council, these committees focus on developing curricula, adapting programs to workforce needs, and identifying strategies to increase student enrollment. Members of the program advisory committees may also attend Chancellor's Advisory Council meetings to listen, but they rarely participate in these more high-level, strategic conversations. The program advisory committees also include representatives from Student Services to ensure students are being supported holistically. For instance, program advisory committees may have education planners from the education center join so that they can advise students using market-responsive data and feedback. Faculty often serve as advisors for specific programs on these committees.

Local Employers' Involvement in Program Design

The involvement of local employers and industry is embedded in every aspect of workforce development, including program development and design.

MARITIME

The development of San Jac's current associate's degree in maritime transportation was driven by industry demand for more qualified mariners. Specifically, employers expressed a demand for more candidates who possessed both technical mariner skills and management skills that were necessary for mariner leadership positions. After reviewing the United States Coast Guard (USCG) approval requirements, the college built a noncredit certification program and an associate's program that would prepare students to join the labor force or transfer to a neighboring four-year institution. San Jac identified key skills including basic safety training and supplemented these core skills with other soft skills such as teamwork and management to develop a well-rounded curriculum.

After success in the noncredit program, San Jac went back to the program advisory committees to get their approval before developing a credit-bearing program that combined USCG-approved and Standards of Training, Certification, and Watchkeeping (STCW)–approved maritime training.[19]

"The Maritime program at San Jacinto College taught me real-life application in the field I was getting my degree in. When I graduated, I was ready for the workforce immediately with the knowledge that allowed me to apply for numerous opportunities."

—*Miles Douglas, Alumnus of the Maritime Transportation Associate's Degree Program*[22]

The program is based in the Maritime Technology and Training Center, a forty-five-thousand-square-foot waterfront facility that is equipped with state-of-the-art bridge and engine room simulators.[20] The resources in the center help the college facilitate more than seventy USCG- and STCW-approved courses. The maritime program offers a solution to the shortage of Gulf Coast mariners as it is developed through strong industry and community partnerships. These efforts were rewarded when the San Jac won the prestigious 2019 Bellwether Award in Workforce Development.[21]

PETROCHEMICAL

Being located in the heart of the largest petrochemical manufacturing complex in the United States, San Jac recognized industry demand for workers with skills in the petrochemical industry as well. By collecting feedback from employers and involving them in the program design and curriculum development stage, San Jac was able to prioritize coursework that would prepare graduates for the jobs that await them after graduation. The leadership team participated in the Chancellor's Advisory Council as well as the program advisory committee to make sure that the program also supported energy and technology market demand through relevant design, curriculum programming, and hands-on learning opportunities.[23] Now, San Jac is the largest producer of petrochemical graduates in the country and helps the region maintain its status as the "energy capital of the world."[24]

In this program, students have access to hands-on training experiences as they work on their associate's degrees and industry certifications. Through a generous $5 million donation and additional support from LyondellBasell, an employer in the region, San Jac created the LyondellBasell Center for Petrochemical, Energy, and Technology as a teaching and learning center for the school. There are more than ninety companies that operate 132 plants within a thirteen-mile radius of the center,[25] and because employers like Lyondell-Basell have a presence at the center, students engage in professional development and networking opportunities on an ongoing basis.

INFORMATION TECHNOLOGY AND SUPPLY CHAIN MANAGEMENT

In partnership with the local petrochemical industry, as well as other industry sectors, San Jac has established two Chancellor's Advisory Councils for cyber-security/iCloud computing and for global and supply chain management. The two councils help the college sharpen its strategic focus on understanding and meeting workforce needs in the region by engaging senior management leaders in these industries. With the Bureau of Labor Statistics predicting high growth for jobs in these industries, expanding programs in these areas will help San Jac support regional economic growth.

AEROSPACE

San Jac's close proximity to Houston—home to NASA's largest research and development facility and employing nearly three thousand federal civil service workers and more than fourteen thousand contract personnel[26]—prompted discussions with local employers about establishing a presence at the Houston Spaceport. These conversations eventually turned into the development of San Jac's aerospace program. Based on a local employer's presentation on the skills and qualifications they sought in future employees and conversations in the Chancellor's Advisory Council and program advisory committee, San Jac leadership developed a curriculum that would equip students with in-demand technical and soft skills. San Jac focused on one skill or topic area and developed coursework and assignments that would prepare the student in each of those skills. The program advisory committee worked with local employers to develop modules that would help prepare students with a composite set of in-demand skills. The group also met monthly to identify ways in which the program could be improved.

The aerospace program is housed at San Jac's EDGE Center, which is the official education training partner for the Houston Spaceport at Ellington Airport. San Jac's aerospace program equips students with experience in electrical, design, manufacturing, operating, and maintenance tracks, and offers technical certificate

"This facility is at the epicenter of the Houston Spaceport. This is where the next chapter of the rivalry to space will be written by the minds and hands of Houstonians for generations to come. The talent who will learn how to build towards the future of space exploration starts right here at the EDGE Center."

—*Mario Diaz, Director of Aviation at the Houston Airport System*[28]

programs that help students advance their careers with coursework in manufacturing and automation, electrical and electronics, and drones. San Jac is now the training partner for the Houston Spaceport as it offers five certification programs that directly support the space and drone industry in the region.[27]

NURSING

By working with hospitals and small clinics in the region, leadership at San Jac developed a bachelor of science degree in nursing (BSN) program and chose to launch it as a hybrid nursing program. This was in response to the demand for nurses with an advanced degree to meet the needs of an aging population,[29] and as a response to the health services industry cluster growing significantly in recent years; it now accounts for nearly 11 percent of Houston's workforce.[30]

To qualify for the BSN program, students must have their associate's degree in applied sciences, hold a registered nurse certification, and be currently employed as a nurse. The program is designed for working, associate's degree–holding nurses to gain an additional credential through hybrid coursework, and it helps identify strong nurses to address regional and national shortages.[31]

After the early success of the BSN program, employers are requesting that San Jac launch new programs within the healthcare industry. Instead of launching certificates in the field, San Jac is using employer feedback to direct efforts to launch new degree programs.

PARTNERSHIPS WITH OTHER COLLEGES TO ADVANCE THE REGIONAL ECONOMY

In the last few years, San Jac has received requests from other community colleges to learn from its experience and replicate the success that the college has had through the Workforce and Economic Development Council. San Jac has granted these requests as it too can learn from the experiences of other colleges to make improvements on its campus.

"In the last few years, we have dropped the scarcity model of competing with other community colleges in the area. Instead, we have realized that our work to build strong workforce partnerships in the region will benefit us, other community colleges, and the local economy. So, if we do our part to grow the workforce, we'll contribute to economic development in the region. One college alone cannot make this difference to workforce development, so we need to embrace working with other community colleges to advance this mission," said Harris.

PARTICIPATION IN REGIONAL WORKFORCE INITIATIVES

San Jacinto is also represented on the subcommittees and boards of different workforce initiatives, including the Economic Alliance Houston Port Region and the Bay Area Houston Economic Partnership. Chancellor Hellyer has served as board chair of both organizations and is on the Executive Council of Upskill Houston. Harris chairs the Workforce Development Committee of the Economic Alliance Houston Port Region and serves on the Workforce Development Committee for the East Harris County Manufacturers Association.[32] Her work with Greater Houston Partnership's UpSkill Houston, the Aspen Institute's Communities that Work Partnership, and Texas Talent Pipeline Management has also greatly influenced workforce development efforts.[33]

SUPPORTING STUDENT SUCCESS

In 2009, leaders at San Jac made organizational and staffing changes to improve student success. The college transitioned to a more centralized leadership structure to ensure alignment of policies and practices across growing campuses. It also redesigned the department chair position to increase focus on instructional improvement. San Jac also implemented a performance management system for all employees to align individual roles and performance to the college's overall goals and values.[34]

San Jac also began to move toward developing a culture of innovation by encouraging faculty and staff to experiment with new approaches to support students without fear of being penalized for failure. For example, leadership at San Jac created Framework Fridays to offer weekly forums for faculty, staff, and administrators to plan reforms and participate in professional development focused on student success. These meetings rotated between different campuses, thereby promoting communication, learning, and collaboration across different parts of the college. Student focus groups conducted after Framework Fridays found that advisors and faculty were better aligned to support students after increased interaction.[35]

Similar to many other colleges, San Jac currently uses different student management systems to track students who are completing credit-bearing and non-credit-bearing coursework. Credit-bearing courses count toward a certificate or a degree, while non-credit-bearing courses are typically used to gain job skills or for continuing education. San Jac recently identified the integration of credit-bearing and non-credit-bearing courses as an area of improvement for the institution. Going forward, it aims to move toward a student onboarding process that brings all students into the university through one door. To make this possible, advisors would need to be trained to serve as a one-stop shop for helping students navigate their time at the institution as all students, regardless of their credit status, would go through the same student navigation system. This would also enable students to transition from non-credit to credit-bearing coursework more easily.

Becoming One College

In the past, San Jac's different campuses and centers often operated in isolation from each other, forcing students to navigate complicated, often conflicting, requirements and policies. To improve alignment, campus president positions were transitioned to provost positions with a direct reporting line to Dr. Laurel Williamson, the Deputy Chancellor and College President. San Jac also increased collaboration between the Academic Affairs and Student Services offices, which historically operated independently. The Provost's Communication Council included representatives from Student Services at each campus and met once a month. This transition to a more coordinated, ongoing, and cross-department collaboration offers more consistent policies and practices across the college and streamlines students' experiences.[36]

Today, San Jac aims to continue removing silos and operate as a single entity despite its many campuses, centers, and programs. To advance its goal of offering a unified student experience, San Jac recently created a temporary position to increase coordination across the college and provide consistency and alignment across credit-bearing and non-credit-bearing programs. In the near future, San Jac aims to create a model of advising in which students can easily transition from noncredit to credit-bearing programs.

"San Jacinto College is always improving. The college has comprehensively restructured its systems to align everything to students' success, from before they enroll until they complete a degree. The college is also especially effective in building relationships with employers to deliver what the community needs to thrive and ensuring that graduates succeed in the workforce," said Joshua Wyner, the executive director for the Aspen Institute College Excellence Program.[37]

Before 2013, department chairs were short-term appointed faculty members who maintained a full teaching load. Leaders recognized the need for department chairs to focus on instructional and program improvement and transitioned to hiring full-time, permanent faculty for these roles. Department chairs would only teach one course a year and instead focus their time on instructional improvement, observing classes, coaching faculty, overseeing program reviewing, and organizing professional development for faculty.[38]

The college also increased collaboration between college leadership and departmental chairs by including deans and members of the executive administration in annual department chair meetings. This integration between the academic and administrative units on campus demonstrated that student success was both an individual and organizational goal. During these meetings, organizational leaders review data on academic program effectiveness, set operational goals, and identify plans to achieve these goals.[39]

Decline in General Studies Majors

San Jac had historically struggled to identify and understand gaps in student outcomes due to its limited institutional research (IR) capacity. In 2008, the college expanded its IR office and established protocols to analyze student data. The college reviewed student success data in gateway English and math courses and data on student outcomes by college majors. This analysis identified that students who majored in general studies had lower levels of success in the labor force (e.g., job opportunities, wages, career progression) in comparison to students who majored in a specific academic discipline. College leaders combined insights from this analysis with research on guided pathways that suggested that well-defined pathways and student-focused support could improve college completion and postgraduation student outcomes. In particular, the college analyzed high-wage jobs in the Houston region and focused efforts to direct students to pursue academic pathways that lead them towards high-paying jobs.[40] Interviews with college leaders suggested that these steps directed students toward in-demand career fields, allowing the college to reduce the number of general studies majors from 23 percent to 14 percent over five academic years (see table 5.2).

San Jac organized its programs into eight *metamajors*, or areas of study, but referred to these as *academic and career pathways* to make them accessible to students and employers alike. It also worked with local school districts to align these pathways to the Texas high school *endorsements*, career fields that students select before high school, so that students and counselors can connect high school courses to pathways at San Jac and beyond. Each pathway was mapped to lead to either transferring to a four-year institution or employment in an in-demand regional job.[41] By mapping academic programs to career pathways and mapping these pathways to the entire student experience, the college is working toward removing barriers for students so they can complete their degree programs and find jobs after graduation.

Efforts to Align Credit and Noncredit Courses

As a part of the Texas Association of Community Colleges (TACC) and the Texas Reskilling and Upskilling through Education (TRUE) initiative, the

TABLE 5.2 Decline in general studies

	Number of awards by academic year					
Type	*2015–2016*	*2016–2017*	*2017–2018*	*2018–2019*	*2019–2020*	*2020–2021*
General studies	1,608	1,349	1,216	990	997	988
Not general studies	5,411	6,151	6,276	6,664	6,138	6,193
Total	7,019	7,500	7,492	7,654	7,135	7,181
	Number of awards by academic year					
Type	*2015–2016*	*2016–2017*	*2017–2018*	*2018–2019*	*2019–2020*	*2020–2021*
General studies	22.90%	18.00%	16.20%	12.90%	14.00%	13.80%
Not general studies	77.10%	82.00%	83.80%	87.10%	86.00%	86.20%

Source: San Jacinto College

college has begun to participate in a noncredit-to-credit alignment lab. Noncredit courses offer students in-demand skills sought by employers and support the college's workforce development mission. Further, noncredit courses often serve as a bridge to enrollment for credit-bearing courses. But as most colleges operate noncredit programs separately from credit programs, the disconnect in policies and systems between the two programs poses a barrier and creates confusion for students. After conducting a self-assessment, San Jac is working to build an action plan that can help the college identify and eliminate barriers to integrating noncredit and credit-bearing courses. San Jac also aims to build visual maps or pathways for students to understand how they can transition from noncredit to credit-bearing programs. This integration process will move the college toward its goal of providing all students with the same support services, regardless of their credit status.

Noncredit Programs as Incubators for Credit Programs

Leaders at San Jac believe that noncredit academic programs can quickly respond to changes in the labor market and feedback from employers as they are not bound by the rigid processes that the credit academic programs must go through. For this reason, it is important to protect the unique values of noncredit programs that allow them to be market-responsive and serve as incubators for credit-bearing programs. The development of a new credit-bearing program requires the college to conduct research, develop white papers, and identify future trends in the industry. This lengthy process can take a few years. Noncredit programs, on the other hand, can be offered sooner due to differences in their budget structure. They operate in a somewhat entrepreneurial manner as they must produce the revenue to cover the costs. This means that the college only launches a program if its analysis indicates that it can carry the program for a year or two and generate revenue. Further, as San Jac works with employers to develop curricula and often hires experts from the industry to teach courses, the college continues to refine these programs even after launching them.

"We believe in taking responsible risks. We do our homework to understand regional and local market demand, form trusting relationships with reliable partners who believe in our ability, and take responsible risks that have small initial investments and exit strategies. San Jac has had many programs

Collective Regional Efforts to Launch New Programs

"San Jacinto College recognizes the opportunity for noncredit and shorter-term programs to offer specific technical skills that ultimately help students get better jobs," said Peter Beard, senior vice president for regional workforce development, Greater Houston Partnership. San Jac's successful programs often start as joint efforts among the college and regional partners that test the educational and labor market benefits through noncredit programs.

San Jac's maritime program initially started as a collective venture between Port Houston, Houston Pilots, some local maritime companies, and the college, with support from the state workforce commission and legislators who advocated for funds to establish maritime training on the Houston Ship Channel. To launch training rapidly, San Jac initially purchased a USCG-approved curriculum from a private maritime training company, and Houston Pilots provided a million-dollar simulator that was housed in a temporary metal building and training facility.

After three years of operation, San Jac was staffed and positioned to develop its own curriculum and receive USCG approval. Although the program was not originally a credit-bearing program, faculty developed a curriculum for the associate of applied science degree in maritime transportation, which was approved by the Texas Higher Education Coordinating Board.

A similar process was employed for the aerospace program, where the local economic development corporation, regional employers, and government entities collectively identified the need for more workforce training in the region. The Houston Airport System provided space for operations, the Bay Area Houston Economic Partnership brought many partners to the program, and the partners helped develop a curriculum and identify faculty. Collaboration with key stakeholders in the local and regional labor market has resulted in students having internships working with companies that are building the lunar landing module and making the spacesuits for the International Space Station.

where students start on the noncredit track and quickly realize the benefits of the program and transition over to the for-credit side," said Harris.

Credit for Prior Experience

Leaders spent the spring of 2022 reviewing San Jac's policies on credit for prior learning. Credit for prior learning recognizes the life experiences of adult learners and translates these experiences into college-level coursework and academic credit. When San Jac reviewed its policies, it identified many challenges and barriers that were preventing students from receiving credit for their work before San Jac. For example, students were required to complete a paid application process to convert the prior learning to academic credit. This additional financial burden prevented many students from going through the process. Reviewing these policies made the leadership team realize that they needed to be more intentional about how a student navigates different student services to allow students to easily find answers to their questions. San Jac is now planning to evaluate its student systems to place the student at the center and best support them in their time at and beyond the college.[42]

FACULTY INCORPORATE AN INDUSTRY-FOCUSED MINDSET

Faculty play an important role in identifying what courses lead to jobs and degrees for students. They study labor market data to identify if courses at San Jac are helping prepare students for jobs in the region and if these jobs offer family-sustaining wages. Faculty often meet employers from their industry to identify opportunities for improvements in their academic programs. For instance, because employers in petrochemical were hiring students before they finished their certificates, they were often not prepared for employment. Upon learning this, faculty met with industry leaders to identify in-demand skills and gaps in student learning. Through conversations with employers, San Jac faculty learned that they should rearrange student progression in the program to have students complete chemistry coursework before completing more hands-on work. This helped align the coursework to jobs in the local labor market and better prepare students to take on employment. Faculty at San Jac also teach students the "culture of the workforce" so that students understand what it means to work in specific industries and are prepared to join the workforce after graduation. The strong relationships that San Jac faculty and leadership share with employers and the industry allow them to adapt to the changing needs of the industry.

Many faculty at San Jac complete externships with local employers during the summer months so that they can learn the most in-demand technical skills and identify opportunities to incorporate these skills into the course curriculum. This also helps faculty understand and incorporate the employer or business mindset into their programs.

Professional Development

Interviews with administrators confirm that San Jac perceives regional employers as the experts on workforce development. The college therefore recruits senior leaders from key industries to build credibility and bring industry expertise to the institution. For example, Jim Griffin, who serves as the associate vice chancellor and executive vice president for the Center for Petrochemical, Energy, and Technology, spent over thirty years in the petrochemical industry, serving as an environmental, health, and safety engineer, a corporate director, and a plant manager for global corporations. In his role prior to joining San Jac, Griffin served as chairman of the board for the East Harris Manufacturers Association. His leadership in the petrochemical industry and his work in the Gulf Coast region positioned him uniquely to improve programs, grow faculty, and build relationships with companies in the region. Executive leadership at San Jac believes that the background, experiences, and expertise that these industry leaders bring to the workforce development efforts are critical to San Jacinto's success as a workforce development provider.

Key Performance Indicators

Leaders at San Jac report workforce development and student success to be integral components of the college's strategic plan. San Jac aims to be the preferred workforce and economic development partner in the region and a champion of lifelong learning. Therefore, annual performance reviews evaluate whether all employees, including faculty, embrace the college's values and mission in their work. Employees are not only measured on individual goals but also assessed on how they prioritize student success and whether they embed workforce development into their everyday work. Their contributions to advancing San Jac's mission are critical to both individual and organizational success.

All employees at the college set personal KPIs that assess their performance against KPIs that directly align with San Jac's annual priorities and that advance student success.[43] For example, the dean of Health and Natural Sciences/Nursing said that building clinical affiliations is included as a KPI for staff in the healthcare and natural sciences. Each employee is encouraged and evaluated on the number and quality of partnerships they establish.

San Jac leaders consider its people to be their biggest asset and are focused on employee growth and development through investments in training and professional development. Interviews with staff across the organization indicate that the collegiate and community-focused culture at San Jac contributes to high rates of employee retention and return.

THE STUDENT EXPERIENCE

Career and Academic Exploration for New Students

During their first semester at the college, students complete assessments of their values, interests, talents, and needs. These assessments examine how certain students are feeling about their metamajors or majors before they meet with admissions advisors and register for classes. Students complete gateway math and English courses in their first semester and begin to participate in career development early. Once students identify an academic pathway, they receive individual counseling to guide them through the academic progression.[44] Students who are interested in transferring to a four-year institution also map out the courses they want to take while at San Jac and the courses they wish to take once they have transferred to the four-year institution. This process of mapping courses to semesters and academic years is specific to an individual's career and degree aspirations. Throughout their time at San Jac, students participate in ongoing career conversations that increase their career awareness and readiness.

San Jac also uses academic planning software that allows every student to create an individualized educational plan based on program maps. This tool allows students and advisors to track their progress and use a "what if" feature to explore alternative program paths.[45]

During their first year, students are required to complete a mandatory student success course that prepares them to be successful in college and connects them to opportunities at San Jac through sustained intervention and advising. The course focuses on key skills including time management, career assessment, advising, educational planning, and instruction.

"Students have many options when making decisions about college. Whether they are new high school graduates, returning students, or students who want to advance in or change their careers, the choices in the Houston area are vast and varied. We are a college that cares. We prioritize student success by providing access and support that lead to equity for all students," said Williamson.

Guided Pathways

Since 2017, San Jac has been involved with pathways work, being selected as one of the original members of the American Association of Community Colleges Pathways project. The following year, San Jac joined Texas Pathways. Working with the University of Houston Guided Pathways to Success (UH GPS) program soon followed. While Houston is among the largest, most rapidly growing metro regions in the country, low postsecondary attainment threatens its economic growth. UH GPS aims to increase postsecondary degree attainment and regional economic growth by offering a pathway for students transferring from Houston area community colleges to four-year universities.[46]

San Jac implemented *guided pathways*, a framework that maps student goals to an academic path, to redesign academic programs and student support services. Faculty, staff, and administrators across different campuses mapped San Jac's academic programs and processes to the student experience to identify barriers to student success. San Jac remapped programs and redesigned student support services to eliminate barriers and increase coordination across the college.

Furthermore, San Jac integrated guided pathways into rethinking developmental education. After identifying math competencies that students need to succeed in its programs, at four-year transfer institutions, and in the workforce, San Jac created four math pathways that align with students' metamajors. It also redesigned its mathematics courses using a corequisite development education model. These corequisite courses are jointly taught by college-level and developmental math instructors for the first college-level course in each pathway. Instead of traditional, prerequisite developmental courses, *corequisite* models enroll students directly into college-level courses and offer them concurrent academic support. Using this model of offering additional support, students move from precollege developmental courses to college-level math courses in one or two semesters. These math courses are aligned to a student's academic and professional pathway, so it prepares them with relevant math skills.[47]

San Jac includes accelerated college preparatory courses, including integrated reading and writing (INRW) courses that combine five courses into two. Students who completed the INRW courses had a 67 percent success rate in first-year English courses, compared to students who took reading and writing courses separately and had a 52 percent success rate.[48]

"The college has made significant investments in guided pathways reforms, ensuring that students receive strong, consistent advising to help them stay on track to completion," said Wyner.[49]

Transfer Pathways

In recent years, San Jac has focused efforts on building and sustaining transfer pathways to support students transitioning to four-year institutions. This goal relates to the college's student success and workforce development mission as it helps students graduate with a credential that prepares them for the workforce.

San Jac leaders seem to have taken concrete steps as a part of the regional initiative to create a seamless pathway for students interested in transferring to four-year colleges. Faculty, department chairs, and deans at San Jac regularly meet with leaders at regional four-year institutions. This alignment between San Jac and its counterparts at four-year institutions ensures that courses and degree pathways translate across the two types of institutions. Communication with four-year institutions has enabled leaders at San Jac to identify misalignments in courses and make programmatic adjustments. For instance, leaders reported that faculty at San Jac changed course syllabi, assignments, and textbooks to ensure students are prepared for academic work when they transition to four-year institutions.

The college has identified expanding transfer opportunities as a goal by reviewing articulation

> "San Jacinto College takes responsibility for not just making sure that its students earn a degree or credential, but also that they succeed after graduation. That care and commitment has yielded great outcomes for graduates."
>
> —*Linda Perlstein, Director at the Aspen Institute College Excellence Program*[50]

agreements and eliminating transfer barriers. San Jac plans to create program-level articulation agreements that identify and delineate specific courses, barriers, and solutions for success within program pathways. Today, San Jac is one of the largest feeders to the University of Houston-Clear Lake, and many of its students also attend the University of Houston-Downtown.

Student Outcomes After Graduation

San Jac's commitment to its students does not end at the point of graduation: the college tracks student outcomes after graduation to study how students perform after leaving the college. Partnerships with four-year institutions and the Texas Workforce Commission allow administrators at San Jac to track student outcomes during their time at the college, at transfer institutions, and in the labor force. Through these partnerships, San Jac has student data on employment status, dates of employment, and salaries. While the college does not currently have data on student job titles, administrators in the IR office are working to get access to this data.

San Jac's ability to form strong partnerships with employers and government agencies that rely on mutual trust and respect allows the institution to receive honest feedback on how students are performing. And it seems that the college does not stop at collecting feedback. Instead, it uses this feedback to improve programs and practices that improve student success and outcomes.

As Williamson puts it, "We want our students to know that there is support and assistance along their path here at San Jac. From admissions and career planning to financial aid guidance and faculty advising, we have staff who will help students complete what they came here to start. Our work in curriculum design and delivery, learning and teaching, and student support systems is making a difference, and it is rewarding for our entire college to be recognized for these efforts."[51]

FOCUS ON EQUITY

Eliminating Financial Barriers

San Jac has made important strides in helping students finish their academic programs. The college recently transitioned to a simplified tuition model that eliminates registration fees and adopts a per-credit-hour rate. This option helps students better plan their educational expenses without additional unexpected financial obstacles. The Open Books educational resource program also offers students access to free and low-cost textbooks and digital course materials, which has saved students more than $6.5 million in textbook costs over three years.[52]

After receiving a donation from philanthropist and author MacKenzie Scott, any student has the opportunity to attend San Jac full-time as a Promise Scholar if they live within San Jac's taxing district at the time of high school graduation. These students have three years to complete their degree. This donation was also used to create the 21Forward scholarship, which provided free tuition to class of 2021 graduates from six independent school districts within the taxing district.

As Hellyer remarked, "We know that finances are often a barrier for students when obtaining their higher education credential; so, our goal is to help remove that barrier while putting students on a path to complete their credential, whether a certificate or degree."[53]

Role of Equity in the Strategic Plan

San Jac's annual priorities for 2021–2022 include expanding its equity focus and commitment. San Jac will continue to analyze disaggregated data to look at how existing instructional and student support, business practices, policies, initiatives, and programming address equity and inclusion and identify any related gaps—something that the college has been doing for over a decade to understand student success as a result of its involvement with Achieving the Dream. After identifying these gaps, San Jac develops strategies to address the student performance and outcome gaps by building the necessary infrastructure and support systems. San Jac also plans to develop key steps that enhance inclusivity in classrooms and learning, review the curriculum for training the workforce and preparing students for the workforce, and achieve equity in student outcomes through programs and courses for different demographic groups. Leaders should also implement strategies that reduce unconscious bias, eliminate implicit bias, and increase diversity in the recruitment, hiring, and retention of employees.[54]

Diversity, Equity, and Inclusion Committees

San Jac believes that when students or employees feel excluded from the learning community, they disengage from their studies and work, which impacts both individual-level performance and goals, and larger organizational goals and initiatives. Therefore, diversity, equity, and inclusion (DEI) committees are focused on student and employee engagement and support.

The Council on Diversity, Equity, and Inclusion includes multiple sub-committees that focus on different functions, including curriculum, student employment outcomes, workforce programs, student engagement and activities, professional development, and policy language. The subcommittees include deans, faculty, student success services, teaching and learning experts, and students. These subcommittees develop and report qualitative and quantitative metrics to examine San Jac's process toward its education, equity, and excellence goals.[55]

The council includes three subcommittees that directly address workforce development programs: (1) student employment outcomes that address hiring and salaries of graduates one year and four years after graduation; (2) program outcomes that disaggregate student performance and completion in various programs by race, ethnicity, gender, and socioeconomic status; and (3) curriculum, which examines course content and activities in workforce programs.

Mentoring Programs

San Jac launched a mentoring program called Intentional Connections to offer guidance and mentoring for underserved student groups who would benefit from extra support. The program places high-risk students in a learning community, which includes college preparatory English and reading, the student success course, and structured career exploration. After students select a field of study for a specific career path, they receive a faculty mentor from that area and visit program courses and activities to ensure that a specific career is the right fit for them. This faculty mentor helps students identify a chosen career path, identifies goals, creates an educational path, and evaluates their educational strengths and weaknesses. After the assessment process, mentors connect students to administrators and faculty members. Students can then "test drive" different programs to see if the program is a good fit before enrolling in a full-semester course.[56]

In 2019, San Jac launched Mosaic, replacing earlier programs that had been designed to support underrepresented students. The mission of the Mosaic program is to support African American and Black-identifying students who enroll at San Jac through a mentoring and bridge program that connects students with faculty and staff who have shared the same life and educational experiences.[57] Students learn about the culture of higher education and connect with resources that enhance their success in college. They also form a community and have opportunities for social engagement with other students and mentors.

San Jac is also recognized for its work with veterans. In addition to offering services at the Center of Excellence for Veteran Student Success, the college also has veteran success coordinators who help transition service members from military to school and into the workforce.

Financial Literacy

The Aid Like a Paycheck program provides students with financial aid refunds every two weeks, instead of a lump-sum payment thirty days after the semester begins.[58] While most financial aid programs offer lump-sum payments, this initiative also offers financial literacy as students are better able to manage their financial resources throughout the semester. This helps students in learning key financial literacy skills that help them remain enrolled and graduate, but also have benefits beyond graduation. Students have access to formal financial literacy and coaching from their entry to San Jac to graduation as well.

DATA USE TO INFORM DECISION-MAKING

Since the formation of the IR office, data now informs all decisions made at the college. For instance, San Jac publishes an open-source strategic measures dashboard on its website to examine student success measures such as retention rates, transfer rates, graduation rates, and awards.

San Jac tracks its students while they are at the college and connects this data to student outcomes data that it receives from the Texas Workforce Commission. Connecting data from these two sources allows the college to understand student success and outcome trends while at the college and beyond. The Texas Workforce Commission offers data on students' employers, salaries, and dates of employment. This data is then made accessible to individuals across all levels of leadership at the

> "These efforts, along with many more, are truly working here at San Jacinto College. Many of these programs and initiatives came directly from our faculty, and we are seeing the results in the classroom and at the end of the year when we celebrate our graduates at commencement."
>
> —*Dr. Brenda Hellyer, Chancellor of San Jacinto College*

college. But San Jac identified gaps in its data, including missing information on job titles; the college is working with the Texas Workforce Commission to fill this data gap and classify employers into specific fields. San Jac is also interested in tracking internship-to-job conversion rates.

Recently, San Jac released an internal-facing dashboard that includes information on student transfer rates, college awards, and retention rates. This data can be disaggregated based on on-campus location, race and ethnicity, gender, Pell Grant status, first-generation indicators, and whether a student is part-time or full-time. Because these metrics influence student success metrics, it is important to disaggregate data to identify where and how to make improvements, at both the institution and programmatic levels.

The Institutional Research and Data Science team regularly compiles student data to share with the chancellor and vice chancellor for strategic initiatives. This data is critical to making important policy recommendations.

As mentioned earlier, San Jac has several DEI committees, including a committee that specifically focuses on workforce development.[59] A representative from the Institutional Research and Data Science team serves on this committee and creates reports that explore how the demographic characteristics in each academic program compare to the demographics of the larger college population. For instance, the committee compares demographic characteristics in individual academic programs to the college's majority Latino student population to see if programs are accurately representing the larger student population at the institution. Because representation from traditionally underrepresented groups is an important step, San Jac works to help students see themselves in industries where they are traditionally underrepresented.

Data is an important component of the program advisory committees as well. As shared earlier, the program advisory committees ask employers about how graduates from San Jac perform after graduation and whether graduates from the college entered these roles prepared for the workforce. Employers are encouraged to give feedback and offer recommendations to San Jac. The program advisory committee also helps the college identify employers who are hiring graduates and employers who are paying the highest wages so that the college can prioritize relationships with employers.

Furthermore, San Jac uses data to determine whether to sunset academic programs, in addition to analyzing enrollment trends, completion rates, labor market trends, and salaries in the region for graduates of those programs. If the college's board approves the recommendation to close a program, the sunsetting process must include creating a plan for students who are currently enrolled in that program.

Incorporating Stakeholder Feedback

San Jac actively collects feedback from students, alumni, and employers in the industry to improve programs, partnerships, and experiences. At the end of each semester, students are asked to complete a survey that aims to learn about their experience with the curriculum and identify opportunities for improvement. Through participation in the Chancellor's Advisory Council and program advisory committees, the college collects feedback from alumni of the program.

San Jac reaches out to alumni across different programs to collect feedback on how their program at the college influenced their preparedness to enter the workforce and to identify skills that should be integrated into the curriculum to improve its efficacy. Because alumni from the program are most often employed at local employers or industry partners, alumni offer feedback on an ongoing basis.

Although San Jac does not have a systematic structure for college employer feedback, the college's focus on continuous improvement has enabled it to encourage employers to share ongoing feedback and quickly respond to employer feedback to make improvements to its programs. The leadership team plans to develop a system to record feedback to ensure it is channeled to the right individuals.

An alumnus of San Jac, who also served on the program advisory committee, raised concerns that the minutes of the meeting do not include a section for feedback. The leadership team immediately included a column in the meeting minutes dedicated to identifying stakeholder feedback and collecting recommendations for improvement. This final column includes feedback from

"When industry and education usually get into the room, they are often speaking different languages. Instead of taking feedback from the industry and engaging in authentic conversations to understand the issues, education often perceives that it has accounted for or anticipated the issue in its program. San Jac is unique because it has a growth mindset in how it solves employer problems and prepares its graduates for employment."

—Peter Beard,
Senior Vice President
for Regional Workforce
Development, Greater
Houston Partnership

employers and alumni to ensure that the feedback is documented and that the next steps are identified. While the program advisory committee previously struggled to retain participants, integrating this mechanism to collect feedback was an important factor in improving retention for the committee. It made participants feel recognized and a part of the process of identifying solutions and opportunities.

CONCLUSION

San Jac's ability to listen to employers, self-reflect on its strengths and limitations, and make improvements based on feedback from key stakeholders has enabled it to support student success after transfer to a four-year institution and in the workforce. The college has built strong partnerships with regional employers, built state-of-the-art training facilities, and eliminated silos to ease student progression and success.

San Jac has an important role to play in developing key industries in the region and influencing economic development. The college has expanded its workforce training efforts to support more industries for growth, including maritime, aerospace, and petrochemicals, by preparing graduates with in-demand skills that make them marketable in the labor force. San Jac has made strong strides in using a data-informed approach to student success and workforce development but should continue to embed ongoing data analysis to make critical decisions relating to program launches and sunsetting. San Jac's goal to place student success and equity at the center of its work will enable the college to remove barriers for students, prepare them for the workforce or to transfer to four-year universities, and make meaningful contributions to the local economy.

"As San Jacinto College heads into the next decade, we will continue to provide students and the community with evolving, innovative, and necessary programs and services that meet the region's needs. Working alongside organizations such as the Bay Area Houston Economic Partnership, we know we can help grow the economy in our region and provide our partners with the talented and skilled workforce they need for decades to come," said Hellyer.[60]

CHAPTER 6

What Will It Take?

Igniting the Community College Engine

Rachel Lipson

When Bob Schwartz and I launched this project back in the fall of 2021, the US labor market stood at a tipping point. The COVID-19 pandemic had exacerbated a long-standing and intersecting set of economic and human capital challenges and brought social inequality to the surface in provocative yet troubling ways. Exacerbating five decades of an expanding gap between rich and poor, the pandemic disproportionately hurt workers without four-year college degrees, workers of color, women, and immigrants. The murder of George Floyd in the summer of 2020 had brought new light to the stubborn and persistent racial wealth gap in America. Meanwhile, an increasingly chaotic global context brought new geopolitical challenges. Rising populism meant more Americans were skeptical toward or outwardly distrustful of perceived elite capture of key institutions like higher education. Pandemic-induced supply chain bottlenecks thrust a wrench in traditional trade relationships and production of many in-demand goods.

To say the least, this context presents a formidable set of challenges for any leader or system to address. And yet, I will argue that we do have one institution in America that is uniquely equipped to meet these challenges head on. In fact, this has been the driving motivation behind this book project. When adequate resourcing is coupled with forward-looking leadership, community colleges can sit in the driver's seat for forging shared prosperity in

America. Our case studies, spanning from Northeast Ohio to the Sunbelt to rural Mississippi, all demonstrate how America's public two-year institutions can effectively tackle some of our country's most pressing social and economic problems.

CONTEXT

We started the research for this book guided by a simple premise: community colleges can play a catalytic role in regional economic development. Because they primarily draw their student body from the surrounding local population, community colleges are inherently rooted in local community and a sense of place. In many rural regions of America, they also represent the only public postsecondary game in town for policymakers and employers looking to upskill their local labor force.

In the past, however, too often, regions have neglected to capitalize on the potential of community colleges. Indeed, as Amy Liu of the Brookings Institution has poignantly argued, many economic development practitioners historically focused near-exclusively on attracting new firms and people.[1] While billions of dollars were spent on tax incentives and business-attraction efforts, relatively little investment was focused on the people and assets already in their locality. The cumulative result has been that the most disadvantaged workers and learners are often left behind.

Yet this moment provides an opportunity to change course and rethink that strategy. At a time when inequality has been accelerating in America, community colleges present a compelling antidote. For decades, because of their affordability and open admissions policies, community colleges have been the most socioeconomically diverse institutions in American higher education. In recent years, we have even more powerful evidence of their role in realizing the American dream. Work from our Harvard colleague Raj Chetty and Opportunity Insights finds that community colleges are responsible for the largest share of *upward mobility success stories*—US students moving from the bottom 20 percent of the income distribution as children to the top 20 percent as adults—of any institution type in the American postsecondary education system. As America faces an impending student debt crisis, the relative affordability and accessibility of community colleges relative to four-year schools makes them an attractive and accessible entry point for millions of learners.

Meanwhile, community colleges have a big role to play in addressing America's racial inequality, which the pandemic brought to the forefront. Data shows that community colleges are consistently the most racially and ethnically diverse segment of American higher education. In addition to serving large shares of Black and Latinx college students, they host English language learning programs that provide entry points for new Americans and recent immigrants. While equity and inclusion continue to present a challenge for the sector, the case studies demonstrate that community colleges are well-positioned to recruit from diverse pockets of their communities.

The changing landscape of globalization also poses an opportunity for community colleges. As competition with China grows fiercer and Russia's war in Ukraine destabilizes trade networks, American manufacturing is in the spotlight. This is an industry in which community colleges, with technical infrastructure, industry-focused faculty, and strong relationships in the market, are uniquely well-placed to take advantage. Our research highlights regions around the country where community colleges are critical to the manufacturing talent supply chain. If any public educational institution is to benefit from the increasing emphasis on supply chain resiliency, it will be the community college system. As Intel breaks ground on a new massive semiconductor chip factory in Ohio this year, the Lorain County Community College (LCCC) mechatronics program is a great example of what is possible when done right.

Finally, since the onset of COVID-19 in March 2020, American higher education faces grave new challenges to its existence. In 2013, 70 percent of US adults said they considered a college education to be "very important." Just six years later, it had fallen to about half.[2] Then the pandemic happened. Strada's Public Viewpoint polling found that the share of American adults who believed that additional education would be "worth the cost" or would "get [them] a good job" declined by over half between 2019 and 2020.[3] As the dominant narrative of bachelor's degrees being the sole and best pathway to economic mobility loses luster, community colleges have an opportunity to respond to these changing attitudes. Across the board in our cases, we found that community colleges do not face the same elitist stigma or out-of-touch stereotypes attached to prestigious four-year universities. Indeed, they may be the only institutions that can restore trust in higher education for large swaths of the US population.

MEETING THE MOMENT

From the shores of Lake Erie to the Arizona desert to the booming DC suburbs to the Mississippi coast, this book describes diverse populations, histories, and growth industries. However, the community colleges in these regions look remarkably alike in one very important way. They are well-respected by employers, policymakers, and civil society in their communities and viewed as absolutely critical to the trajectories of their respective regional economies.

Across the over fifty interviews conducted for this project, stakeholders ranging from CEOs to local policymakers to community-based organizations to industry groups expressed a shared sentiment: these colleges were integral to any regional growth plan. As Tony Gallo, the president and CEO of Lorain County Chamber of Commerce, describes it: "There's not a day that goes by that I probably don't talk to somebody from [the] community college . . . [Our] county has been through a lot of ups and downs as far as businesses closing, moving, and consolidating. [The] college has always been there to say, 'Okay, that was really bad. What do we do to move forward to get past this? . . . I'm grateful every day that Lorain County Community College is here and is [our] partner."

How do these schools do it? They put shared prosperity for their communities at the center of their vision—and then couple external- and internal-facing strategies to achieve it.

BUILDING THE BLUEPRINT: REGIONAL KINGMAKERS

Outward-Facing Leadership

In each of our case study institutions, college senior executive teams sit at the table in key economic decision-making bodies. The chancellors and presidents model their institutions' priorities by dedicating a significant share of attention and time toward externally facing activities. Among other notable examples in their communities:

- In Lorain County, President Marcia Ballinger serves on the board of directors for Northeast Ohio's leading business development organization, Ohio's statewide manufacturing extension partnership, the county's major hospital system, and a leading local financial institution.

- In Pima County, Chancellor Lee Lambert represents the college on boards ranging from Arizona's statewide economic development entity to the region's United Way chapter to Sun Corridor, Inc., a regional alliance of CEOs focused on economic competitiveness.
- In Greater Houston, Chancellor Brenda Hellyer is a board member for organizations including the Center for Houston's Future and the Greater Houston Partnership. She serves as chair of the Board of Directors of the Bay Area Houston Economic Partnership.
- In South Mississippi, President Mary Graham serves on the statewide Workforce Investment Board, as well as the boards of the Gulf Coast Business Council and one of the state's two electric utilities.
- In Northern Virginia, President Anne Kress serves on the boards of the Northern Virginia Chamber of Commerce and the Northern Virginia Technology Council. She has been named to the Virginia Business 500 and the Washington Business Journal Power 100 each year since she joined Northern Virginia Community College (NOVA).

Representation in key strategic entities builds rapport and credibility with employers. But it goes beyond just reputation. These memberships reflect that the college has an important voice and role in codesigning the region's economic vision and priorities.

Effective Targeting of Jobs and Fields that Map to High-Growth and Good-Wage Opportunities

Research consistently shows that picking the right industries and jobs is key if training is to translate into meaningful employment. But this seemingly intuitive insight has often proved difficult to implement in practice. In the case of thriving community colleges, though, there is a consistently strong track record. The institutions in this volume use their strategic planning processes to carefully solicit quantitative and qualitative insights about where labor markets are going. As a result, they are making good bets. In Virginia, NOVA has aligned its strategy to accelerate the growing IT sector in the region. In Ohio, LCCC capitalizes on its anchor industries of healthcare and manufacturing. In Tucson, Pima is racing ahead in growing applied technology fields, including automotive and aviation. The ability to choose well is premised in part on making good use of labor market information. Perhaps even more important, though, is that the colleges make use of their connections on the ground. The leaders participating in regional economic planning entities, alongside faculty with strong industry ties, acquire reliable intelligence about where the economy is going. Then, internally, they create mechanisms to feed that intelligence into the creation, expansion, and, sometimes, closing of programs.

Creative and Collaborative Resourcing: Mobilizing New Capital to Meet Opportunities

One thing that is striking across our cases: the colleges play an active role in all major initiatives to bring good jobs to their region. Working together with other entities in the regional economic development ecosystem, these colleges pull in a combination of federal, state, corporate, and philanthropic resources to support new pipelines into key industries. In Virginia, NOVA's technology programs played an important role in the state's winning bid for Amazon HQ2. In Houston, San Jacinto was a leading entity in the region's recent application to the Department of Commerce's Good Jobs Challenge. In Ohio, LCCC's semiconductor chip manufacturing program was featured prominently in efforts to bring Intel to the state. In Tucson, the governor's office allocated $15 million to the college's Applied Technology Academy to support a growing partnership with Caterpillar. Meanwhile, in Mississippi, a $20 million 2021 gift from MacKenzie Scott to the college will support the region's focus on six high-growth sectors, including the blue economy, healthcare, and transportation. These diversified and collaborative resourcing strategies enable colleges to be proactive rather than reactive to an ever-changing regional business environment.

Deep, Sustained, Long-Term Relationships with Key Regional Employers

Employer engagement is often cited as a critical component to successful workforce training efforts. However, policymakers often struggle to communicate what differentiates a cursory industry advisory board from a true talent supply chain partnership. In each of the case studies, the featured college has built long-term, sustained strategic hiring partnerships with local industry partners. For instance, in Mississippi, an apprenticeship program with Ingalls Shipbuilding at Mississippi Gulf Coast Community College (MGCCC) dates all the way back to the 1950s.

Importantly, though, the best and most scalable employer partnerships do not serve the needs of just one company. Instead, they tap into the needs of key regional clusters. San Jacinto's petrochemical initiative services over ninety companies and 113 plants within a thirteen-mile radius. LCCC's microelectromechanical systems program works with over eighty partner companies. With these types of training models, the colleges become a central connecting node between networks of interconnected companies with shared talent needs.

Activating the Regional Innovation Ecosystem

Forward-looking community colleges increasingly participate in the development of local entrepreneurship ecosystems. The five featured colleges work closely with start-ups to support new business formation in their communities. Some explicitly build innovation centers on campus and create mentorship programs to connect aspiring founders to opportunities in the community. In other contexts, they share modern equipment and space with local companies to support R&D efforts. Both Pima and MGCCC opened centers on campus to provide technical assistance services for small businesses and help incumbent firms grow more jobs for the local economy. This function is especially important in struggling regions where the existing employer base does not provide enough good-paying opportunities at present to keep graduates close to home.

CHALLENGING THE STATUS QUO: INSTITUTIONAL TRANSFORMATION

In addition to looking outward in the community, delivering on a good jobs agenda also requires thoughtful internal practices. In fact, the institutions featured in this volume have all challenged the traditional organizational models and hierarchies of community colleges.

At their best, institutional reform decisions are made with shared prosperity as the north star. This looks different from college to college, but it starts with a high-level vision from the president showing that economic mobility in the community is what staff and faculty are all there to support.

More Integrated Structures to Connect Education and Employment

Many community colleges look remarkably similar in organizational structure to when they opened in the middle of the twentieth century. However, more innovative schools focus on how programs of study and support services can be best structured to be intuitive and user-centered for both students and employers. Our volume features notable college redesign efforts. While unique in each context, the schools have implemented changes to reduce any institutional silos that could detract from the good jobs mission.

Functionally, these reorganization efforts have two primary goals. First, they create more straightforward ways to interface with industry. Employers want to be able to come to the college to help them meet a specific skill or labor need. They are not necessarily invested in whether they should go to a credit or noncredit unit, each with different division heads and procedures. To simplify engagement, reorganization efforts at both NOVA and Pima created new horizontal business development units that could serve as a single-entry point for all employers in the region. The leaders of these cross-college departments then work directly with the employers to determine the best-fit model.

Second, new models aim to take better advantage of the benefits of noncredit programs. Noncredit offerings are usually easier for colleges to start up and therefore can be important tools to respond quickly to new labor demand. Noncredit courses also are often more conducive to hiring adjunct instructors from industry. In Houston, San Jacinto built a nimble model where noncredit programs can serve as incubators for programs that will eventually go on through institutional approval processes and become credit programs. This gives the college some time and space to test and iterate on the offering and ensure the skills are truly in demand in the labor market.

Third, the blurring of credit and noncredit offerings in the college hierarchy creates value for learners. For students, noncredit programs are often shorter in length and closely linked to jobs in industry; therefore, they often represent a more accessible stepping stone into the college. Instead of siloing noncredit learners into a different division, an integrated model can help students avoid the stigma often associated with career and technical education. Meanwhile, bringing the noncredit offerings into the academic corpus of the institution allows the school to leverage synergies across related coursework targeting the same industry—including instructors, employer relations, and navigation. In many cases, this model can create more seamless transitions for learners who start in noncredit courses to continue on an educational pathway and acquire a credential. MGCCC's schools model provides an actionable example of this kind of restructuring.

Flexible On-Ramps and Off-Ramps

Community colleges have always served significant shares of part-time students, but in recent years, schools are innovating to develop additional flexible pathways. Shorter programs in particular are gaining steam, especially given growing competition from online, for-profit, and nonprofit training providers. During the pandemic, some schools started new experiments with six- to twelve-week fast-track programs. At LCCC, the program appears to be a major success. Not only did it attract a new population of adults, but the college also was able to retrain and transition many of these new learners into longer-term programs after completion. NOVA has benefitted for a few years now from the State of Virginia's FastForward program, which links short-term programs in high-demand fields with new subsidies and stipends. Because these programs have a shorter time commitment up front, they appear to reduce barriers to enrollment. In an economy where workers will need continuous upskilling, models like these that facilitate more seamless transitions between education and work provide a promising avenue.

Proactive Career Advising and Student Supports

For colleges to achieve their jobs mission, they need to facilitate good matches between students and employment opportunities. Career planning integrated throughout the entirety of the student life cycle plays an important role in connecting coursework to economic opportunity.

Advising capacity is typically a challenge. Despite strong research backing, advising has traditionally been woefully underfunded at community colleges. The schools in this volume demonstrate creative solutions to increase support for career navigation. Models include training of college faculty and other staff to provide career advising (LCCC), providing career guidance integrated into the classroom (NOVA), and creating cohort-based models and mentorship (MGCCC). San Jacinto is especially impressive here. The college crafted a new approach including a mandatory student success course, new technology for pathway planning, and more individualized advising. As a result, San Jac reduced the share of general studies awards by almost half in just five years. Because general studies associate of arts degrees have notoriously poor labor market outcomes, this kind of effort can go a long way in supporting both students and employers that want to hire them.

In addition to advising, research consistently finds that the same set of factors that often inhibits low-income students from completing a credential also impacts their ability to succeed in the labor market: transportation, food security, housing, caregiving, healthcare access, and financial emergencies. Here, community colleges provide critical services that also benefit the broader community. When colleges invest in wraparound services like food banks, transportation subsidies, and referrals to social services, they also help local employers, who in turn will receive employees better able to be retained on the job.

Negating Opportunity Cost

Employers and learners alike benefit from models where students can learn in environments that more closely mimic the workplace. Earn-and-learn models, like apprenticeships, paid internships, and co-ops, have a strong base in the research evidence. These opportunities are great for attracting students, especially those who can't afford to forgo earnings for an extended period of time and others who are looking to acquire relevant professional experience and connections. But they also work well for local employers facing labor shortages. The model allows them to get the workers they need quickly, without having to wait for the students to complete their programs. And by creating a consistent and sustainable pipeline for entry-level talent, earn and learn can reduce churn in the long run.

Historically, community colleges have struggled to make earn and learn the norm. But the tight labor market at time of writing presents a ripe opportunity. Many of the colleges in this volume have taken advantage and are actively recruiting new earn-and-learn partners. At Pima, the college now guarantees that 100 percent of its learners will have a work-based learning experience, many of which are paid. NOVA, located in a region with a notoriously high cost of living, launched a new IT apprenticeship program with AT&T in 2021. LCCC has expanded its earn-and-learn opportunities to five fields, including new additions in software development and automation engineering. All are looking to grow more.

Data-Driven Culture

Finally, the cases demonstrate how colleges can build cultures and systems where data aids decision-making. While the higher education sector at large is still hindered by the lack of access to employment and wage information, the five schools in our cohort have not waited around for policymakers to fix the problem. NOVA has developed an in-house labor analytics shop. MGCCC has built a detailed dashboard to understand the health of all its job-focused programs. And San Jacinto is one of the only institutions in Texas with a data-sharing agreement for wage records from the Texas Workforce Commission. Even the most well-intended programs sometimes fail. Data has been critical to understand what is working and what needs rethinking.

STEPPING OUT FROM THE SHADOWS: THE NEXT FRONTIER FOR COMMUNITY COLLEGES

Realizing the Reskilling Revolution

Community colleges already reach an older population than other higher education institutions. However, they will need to step up their efforts for the US to realize high productivity growth in coming decades. Good jobs in our economy increasingly require some type of postsecondary credential.[4] Stalled immigration policies and declining birth rates mean both our education and employment systems are hitting a demographic wall. Even absent recent declines in the share of high school graduates enrolling in college, two-year institutions will not and should not rely primarily on the traditional college-going-age population. There is a lot of room for growth here, especially with lower sticker prices and shorter programs. Currently, adults over the age of twenty-two represent less than half of national two-year enrollment.[5]

If community colleges are to capitalize on the opportunity with older learners, what changes will be required? Perhaps the most significant shift, already underway, is toward a focus on the needs of working learners. Meeting their needs requires a rethinking of many internal structures at a college. Many of the colleges featured in this volume have been leading the way in these changes, including in the following areas:

- *More convenient scheduling:* Colleges are offering course availability on the weekends and evenings, as well as program schedules that are aligned directly with timing of paid employment opportunities with local employers in the field of study.
- *Increased availability of remote and hybrid options:* This is especially important in rural areas with long commute times and for women and caregivers who can't leave home. Opportunities to learn from home open up doors to new populations.
- *More integrated, paid work experiences:* As described earlier, apprenticeships, paid internships, and stipends are especially important for adults who can't afford to forgo earnings.

Forging a New Equity Agenda

While community colleges tend to serve a diverse population, that doesn't mean that all community college students have access to equitable opportunities. In fact, the occupational segregation that we see in the broader economy has often been mirrored in community college enrollment. If we are truly to break down generations of intergenerational racial inequality, we will need to focus on disparities inside and across these institutions. The focus on equity, of course, should not neglect traditional outcome metrics like completion and transfer, but it also must extend to consider what happens to students after they leave the institution. If you open up the hood at community colleges, many programs that lead to the best-paying jobs have disproportionately enrolled white men.[6] Breaking down inequitable structures will require more accountability to track demographic metrics at a program level, plus increased outreach and engagement to diverse groups, as MGCCC is prioritizing in its community. Faculty diversity, particularly in workforce-focused programs, should be another priority.

Preparing for the Future of Work

As the economy changes, community colleges will need to keep a finger on the pulse of how structural shifts affect the labor market that their graduates will enter. One clear focus needs to be on ensuring transferable skills. Job-specific training can be very effective, but returns will decrease in the long run if we train for occupations that become obsolete due to technological change.

Research from my colleague David Deming at Harvard shows that social skills are increasing in demand in the labor market. Community colleges will do well for both their students and employers if they can better integrate social skill development (e.g., teamwork, communication, and leadership) into their technical programs.

A second development that community colleges must closely monitor is the changing geography of work. While some regions face risks of job displacement from remote work, for other communities this could become a promising opportunity in the future. As the post-COVID environment of remote and hybrid work stabilizes, innovative community colleges may be able to mobilize remote jobs as a way to combat regional inequality. We may eventually see growing shares of community colleges, especially in economically distressed regions, start to apply a broader lens to the labor market. I will be watching to see if community colleges are able to implement effective remote job-placement strategies and build partnerships with companies based in other parts of the country.

If You Build It, Will They Come?

This volume would be remiss if we did not address the current reality: some community colleges are nearing crisis levels in enrollment declines since the onset of the pandemic. At the time of writing, community colleges nationally had lost over 827,000 students since spring 2020, representing a 16.5 percent dip in enrollment.[7] While enrollment has been down across the whole US postsecondary sector, this represents a larger drop than at public four-year peers.

Observers of the sector have posited a variety of potential explanations. Many center on the overlap between the populations that community colleges serve, the communities most impacted by COVID-19 infections, and the students who were least likely to be able to weather the shift to online learning. Still, the trend line exposes a major challenge for community colleges across the country if they are to win in the twenty-first century.

The numbers call for a conversation about *marketing*, sometimes conceived as a dirty word in higher education. Indeed, in relatively recent history, many US students were abused by for-profit colleges that spent millions on marketing budgets, only to deliver little value on the other side. But it will be impossible for community colleges to realize their shared prosperity potential if they do not invest more in outreach and recruitment. This is especially true given increasing competition from online providers, new social enterprises, and nonprofits, not to mention a very hot labor market.

The five cases present some signs of optimism here, however. Many workforce-focused programs tended to fare better in the past few years, both at our case study schools and in national data. For instance, construction trades enrollment at community colleges was up 19 percent in spring 2022. Other high-growth areas nationally include mechanical repair and computer science. Conversely, liberal arts enrollment at community colleges has been on the decline for three consecutive years.[8] Meanwhile, institutions like NOVA are taking advantage of the strong brands of corporate partners like Amazon to attract new candidates for programs that lead directly to jobs with the employer partner.

As more and more Americans say that they are looking for education that will help them get better jobs, community colleges that can both prove results and build a brand around economic success will be better positioned.

Fixing the Funding Model

This book highlights a set of colleges that have been entrepreneurial and creative in piecing together resources for the "good jobs" mission. Still, the fact remains overall that the funding model for community colleges is broken. Even as they reach some of the nation's hardest learners to serve, two-year institutions receive one-third less in education revenue per student enrolled than four-year institutions.[9] This is in part because they charge much lower tuition and receive minimal research funds. The lack of funding for noncredit programs in particular was raised consistently by many of the stakeholders we interviewed for the cases as an obstacle to realizing colleges' economic development potential.

Given that community colleges draw a large share of their revenue from state and local appropriations, a one-size-fits-all federal solution appears unlikely. However, conversations for this book highlighted at least four potential models that could substantially boost community colleges' shared prosperity mission. These models could all be pursued piecemeal, but they are likely to be more impactful if deployed in some combination at the federal, state, and/or local level.

Funding the Shared Prosperity Mission

1. *The Economic Development Model:* Partnership grants are provided for colleges to work with industry and ecosystem partners.

    Justification:

    Most current funding streams follow the student, not the institution. This is a mechanism to support big bets and investments in high-priority fields and align cross-sector partners toward a shared regional vision.

    Examples:

    -   The Department of Commerce's Good Jobs Challenge and Build Back Better regional grants, funded by the 2021 American Rescue Plan, supported cross-sector partnerships for job training in aligned regional clusters.
    -   The Obama Administration's Trade Adjustment Assistance Community College and Career Training grants, administered by the Department of Labor, invested in grants for community colleges to partner with industry for targeted workforce programs for adults.
    -   California's Career Pathways Trust Fund funded regional consortia to expand career pathways for young people, including high school, community college, and employer partners.

    Challenge:

    Lack of sustainability. Typically, this model is supported by one-time competitions in which funds expire, rather than consistent, reliable funding.

2. *The Short-Term Credential Model:* Financial aid programs are provided for students to pursue and complete short-term programs in high-demand fields at little or no out-of-pocket cost.

    Justification:

    This is a way to close the funding gap for short-term, job-focused programs.

Examples:

- Short-term Pell funding, under consideration by Congress at the time of writing, would extend federal financial aid programs to shorter programs.
- Virginia's FastForward program provides funding for short-term credentials in fields where the state faces significant labor shortages.

Challenge:

Ensuring labor market return. While program quality is a challenge across higher education, some policymakers are particularly concerned with how to ensure that funds for short-term training do not support credentials with minimal returns in the labor market.

3. *The Student Support Model:* Appropriations are given for institutions to provide comprehensive student services and wraparound supports.

   Justification:

   Student services like advising are often the first to go in budgetary downturns, yet we know from research that they are critical for persistence and completion.

   Examples:

   - Ohio's Community College Acceleration Program is a state effort to scale the renowned ASAP model for providing comprehensive wraparound supports (started at the City University of New York) to community college students. The program was recently approved in state appropriations and funded through SNAP Employment and Training dollars.[10]
   - California recently allocated $40 million annually to help its 115 community colleges create centers to support students' basic needs.[11]
   - The federal Community College Student Success Act, under consideration by Congress, would provide more federal funding to support these functions.

Challenge:
Very targeted funding for specific services will not solve the issue of broader resource constraints in community colleges.

4. *The Formula Funding Model:* This model would change the base allocation for annual appropriations.

Justification:
Formula reforms provide levers to tie funding to outcomes.

Potential Options:
- Performance funding can incorporate labor market outcome metrics.
- Enrollment formulas can consider whether a field is in demand and/or the cost of providing more expensive equipment or faculty.
- Equity provisions can account for schools that serve priority, disadvantaged population groups that may be more expensive to serve.[12]

Challenge:
All three options have promise, but selecting the right metrics has been challenging, and evidence on the effectiveness of changes implemented in states to date is still nascent.

Rethinking How We Define Community College Success

This is a moment when we must reconsider how we judge the impact of America's community colleges. Graduation and transfer rates alone can't capture economic opportunity, which is the primary reason so many Americans choose postsecondary education in the first place. Meanwhile, our education accountability system is not built to respond to the ways higher education must adapt in the twenty-first century. Consider just a few examples:

- IPEDS, the national postsecondary education data system, does not cover noncredit learners, who comprise 40 percent of community college students nationally.[13] Yet recent research from Iowa finds that almost two-thirds of noncredit students were enrolled in occupational training.[14] We can't understand the full impact of community colleges' impact on the workforce without considering noncredit paths.

- Many workforce-focused learners at community colleges enroll for just one or a few particular courses. These students never had the intention to graduate, and they view acquisition of the desired skill as a success. Yet their outcomes are counted as a failure for the institution.[15]
- Enrollment-based funding formulas in states tend to rely on full-time student enrollment numbers rather than total headcount—disadvantaging community colleges that serve large shares of part-time students, like parents and adults.[16]

While valiant efforts exist to confront these challenges, the narrative has still not gone mainstream with policymakers and the general public.[17]

Finally, most policymaking and research conceives of the community college from the primary frame of student outcomes. There has been much less effort to measure or enhance the impact of the institution on the surrounding community.[18] But if the US truly is to leverage community colleges as economic development institutions, we need also to understand and improve their effect on local business formation, growth, equality, and prosperity.

If we resource them properly and support effective leaders at the helm, community colleges can become *the* critical institutions that bring shared prosperity to our communities. The pending question is whether our policymakers, businesses, and civic leaders around the country can recognize that potential and mobilize to realize it.

APPENDIX

Our Case Study Institutions
in Context

TABLE 0.1 Our case study institutions: regional comparison

Community college	Community type (1)	US region (2)	Metropolitan statistical area, state (3)	Percent of county residents with at least a bachelor's degree (25 years and older) (4)	Median household income for residents in county (4)
Lorain County Community College	Urban	Midwest	Cleveland-Elyria, OH	25.3%	$58,798
Mississippi Gulf Coast Community College	Rural	Southeast	Gulfport-Biloxi, MS	15.2%	$47,683
Northern Virginia Community College	Suburban	Mid-Atlantic	Washington-Arlington-Alexandria, DC-VA-MD-WV	62.1%	$127,866
Pima Community College	Urban	Southwest	Tucson, AZ	33.6%	$55,023
San Jacinto Community College	Suburban	South	Houston-The Woodlands-Sugar Land, TX	32.3%	$63,022

Sources: (1) College Scorecard, 2021, Geographic Density and City Proximity; (2) US Department of Commerce Economics and Statistics Administration, US Census Bureau, (3) US Department of Housing and Urban Development; (4) US Census Bureau, 2020.

TABLE 0.2 Our case study institutions: socioeconomic comparison

Community college	Total enrollment, academic year 2021–2022 1)*	Percent of students who received Pell Grants, credit only (2)**	Percent of students from the bottom 40% of US income distribution, credit only (3)**	Percent of students from the bottom 20% of US income distribution, credit only (3)**
Lorain County Community College	14,322	53%	31%	14%
Mississippi Gulf Coast Community College	20,282	62%	42%	19%
Northern Virginia Community College	72,798	41%	24%	9%
Pima Community College	33,993	57%	36%	15%
San Jacinto Community College	44,947	40%	34%	13%

Sources: (1) Lorain County Community College, Mississippi Gulf Coast Community College, Northern Virginia Community College, Pima Community College, San Jacinto Community College; (2) College Scorecard, 2021; (3) Raj Chetty, John Friedman, Emmanuel Saez, Nicholas Turner, and Danny Yagan, Mobility Report Cards: The Role of Colleges in Intergenerational Mobility, NBER Working Paper No. 23618, 2017.

*Enrollment data reflects counts of credit, noncredit, and dual enrollment students provided independently by the institutional research offices at each case college. There may be differing data definitions or collection methodologies across institutions that could affect counts."

**College Scorecard and Mobility Scorecard data do not include noncredit students.

TABLE 0.3 Our case study institutions: enrollment by race/ethnicity, 2021–2022 academic year*

Community college	Native American/Alaska Native	Asian	Black/African American	Hispanic/Latino	Native Hawaiian/Pacific Islander	Two or more races	Unknown	White	Non-US resident
Lorain County Community College	47	216	1489	1412	13	620	385	9528	59
Mississippi Gulf Coast Community College	113	433	5684	1330	23	615	1335	10797	0
Northern Virginia Community College	202	12035	10933	15736	2592	3497	1006	25068	357
Pima Community College	570	1016	1718	13602	94	742	1425	10387	0
San Jacinto Community College	0	2769	4649	25593	0	0	3850	8329	0

Sources: Lorain County Community College, Mississippi Gulf Coast Community College, Northern Virginia Community College, Pima Community College, San Jacinto Community College.
*This data reflects total enrollment for each college, which includes both credit and noncredit student enrollment for the 2021–2022 academic year.

NOTES

PREFACE

1. OECD, *Learning for Jobs* (Paris: OECD Publishing, 2010), https://doi.org/https://doi .org/10.1787/9789264087460-en.

INTRODUCTION

1. Victoria Yuen, "The $78 Billion Community College Funding Shortfall," Center for American Progress, October 7, 2020, https://www.americanprogress.org/article/78 -billion-community-college-funding-shortfall/.
2. Quotations from campus interviews and college partners are interspersed throughout the cases. All quotations in come from the interviews conducted by the chapter authors, unless otherwise noted.
3. Robert Schwartz, "Convening: How Community Colleges Can Drive Shared Prosperity," Harvard Project on Workforce, June 29, 2022, https://www.pw.hks.harvard.edu /post/community-college-convening.

CHAPTER 1

1. US Census Bureau, "QuickFacts: Lorain County, Ohio," United States Census Bureau, accessed June 8, 2022, https://www.census.gov/quickfacts/fact/table/loraincountyohio /PST045221.
2. Darwin H. Stapleton, "Industry," in *Encyclopedia of Cleveland History*, Case Western Reserve University, accessed June 8, 2022, https://case.edu/ech/articles/i/industry.
3. Carol Poh Miller, "Iron and Steel Industry," in *Encyclopedia of Cleveland History*, Case Western Reserve University, accessed June 8, 2022, https://case.edu/ech/articles/i/iron -and-steel-industry.
4. "Advanced Manufacturing," Team NEO, 2022, https://northeastohioregion.com /industries/advanced-manufacturing/.
5. Dave Claborn, "Silver Tsunami Washing Over the U.S. Workforce," *Area Development*, May 16, 2017, https://www.areadevelopment.com/skilled-workforce-STEM/workforce -q2-2017/silver-tsunami-washing-over-th-US-workforce.shtml.
6. Paul Wellener and Kate Hardin, "2022 Manufacturing Industry Outlook," Deloitte, https://www2.deloitte.com/us/en/pages/energy-and-resources/articles/manufacturing -industry-outlook.html.
7. "Healthcare & Biomedical," Team NEO, 2022, https://northeastohioregion.com /industries/healthcare-biotechnology/.

8. "Logistics," Team NEO, 2022, https://northeastohioregion.com/industries/logistics/.

9. "Intel Announces Next US Site with Landmark Investment in Ohio," Intel, January 21, 2022, https://www.intel.com/content/www/us/en/newsroom/news/intel-announces -next-us-site-landmark-investment-ohio.html.

10. "Vision 2025: A New Strategic Plan for Lorain County Community College," Lorain County Community College, accessed May 20, 2022, https://www.loraincc.edu/about /vision-2025/.

11. Thomas Bailey, Shanna Smith Jaggars, and Davis Jenkins, *What We Know About Guided Pathways* (New York: Community College Research Center, Teachers College, Columbia University, 2015), https://ccrc.tc.columbia.edu/media/k2/attachments/What-We -Know-Guided-Pathways.pdf.

12. Marisa Vernon-White (vice president for enrollment management and student services, Lorain County Community College), interview in February 2022.

13. "Vision 2025."

14. Terri Sandu (director of talent and business innovation, Lorain County Community College), interview in February 2022.

15. "Small Business Development Center (SBDC)," Lorain County Community College, https://www.loraincc.edu/business/sbdc/.

16. "Northeast Ohio Region: Talent, Innovation, Opportunity, Affordability," Team NEO, 2022, https://northeastohioregion.com/.

17. Marcia Ballinger (president, Lorain County Community College) and Tony Gallo (president and CEO, Lorain County Chamber of Commerce), interviews in February 2022.

18. "Cleveland Manufacturing Advocacy & Growth Network Consultants," MAGNET, https://www.manufacturingsuccess.org.

19. Ethan Karp (president and CEO, MAGNET), interview in February 2022.

20. Kelly Zelesnik (dean of engineering technologies, Lorain County Community College), interview in February 2022.

21. Ballinger, interview.

22. John D. Chamberlain, "Necessary Skills Now: Developing Employability Skills Through Sector-Specific Integrated Scenarios in Information Technology and Advanced Manufacturing," National Science Foundation, Award Abstract #1501990, last modified July 31, 2019, https://www.nsf.gov/awardsearch/showAward?AWD_ID=1501990.

23. Sandu, interview.

24. Cindy Kushner (director of school and community partnerships, Lorain County Community College), interview in February 2022.

25. Tracy Green (vice president, strategic and institutional development, Lorain County Community College), interview in February 2022.

26. "Completion by Design," WestEd, https://www.wested.org/project/completion-by -design/.

27. Kushner, interview in February 2022.

28. Marisa Vernon-White and Thomas Benjamin (institutional research, planning and engagement, Lorain County Community College), interviews in February 2022.

29. Vernon-White and Benjamin, interviews.

30. Hayley Glatter, "Dual Enrollment as an Engine of Economic Mobility: A Q&A with Lorain County Community College President Marcia Ballinger," Community College Research Center, December 8, 2020, https://ccrc.tc.columbia.edu/easyblog/marcia -ballinger-dual-enrollment.html.

31. "College Credit Plus," Lorain County Community College, accessed May 20, 2022, https://www.lorainccc.edu/ccp/.
32. "Building IT Futures," Lorain County Community College, accessed May 20, 2022, https://www.lorainccc.edu/tech-prep/buildingitfutures/.
33. "Fast-Track to Employment Certificates," Lorain County Community College, accessed May 20, 2022, https://www.lorainccc.edu/programs-and-careers/fast-track/.
34. "LCCC Offers Free Fast-Track Employment Certificates," Lorain County Community College, June 22, 2020, https://www.lorainccc.edu/newsroom/lccc-offers-free-fast-track-employment-certificates/.
35. JFF slides provided by Tracy Green (vice president, strategic and institutional development, Lorain County Community College) in an email on May 19, 2022.
36. Kushner and Green, interviews in February 2022.
37. "Earn and Learn—TRAIN OH," Lorain County Community College, accessed May 20, 2022, https://www.lorainccc.edu/programs-and-careers/industry-training/trainoh/.
38. Zelesnik, interview.
39. Kushner, interview.
40. Lee E. Ohanian, "Competition and the Decline of the Rust Belt," Federal Reserve Bank of Minneapolis, December 20, 2014, https://www.minneapolisfed.org:443/article/2014/competition-and-the-decline-of-the-rust-belt.
41. Rolf Pendall, Erika Poethig, Mark Treskon, and Emily Blumenthal, *The Future of the Great Lakes Region* (Washington, DC: Urban Institute, 2017), https://www.urban.org/sites/default/files/publication/89087/great_lakes_0.pdf.
42. "Average Hourly Earnings of Production and Nonsupervisory Employees, Manufacturing," Economic Research, Federal Reserve Bank of St Louis, June 2022, https://fred.stlouisfed.org/series/CES3000000008.
43. Paul Wellener, Heather Ashton, Chad Moutray, and Victor Reyes, "Creating Pathways for Tomorrow's Workforce Today," Deloitte Insights, May 4, 2021, https://www2.deloitte.com/us/en/insights/industry/manufacturing/manufacturing-industry-diversity.html.
44. Wellener et al., "Creating Pathways."
45. Ballinger, interview.
46. Benjamin Preston, "Global Chip Shortage Makes It Tough to Buy Certain Cars," Consumer Reports, last updated June 13, 2022, https://www.consumerreports.org/buying-a-car/global-chip-shortage-makes-it-tough-to-buy-certain-cars-a8160576456/.
47. "Home Page," QED, https://qedinnovations.com/.
48. Johnny Vanderford (program coordinator, mechatronics technology, Lorain County Community College), interview in March 2022.
49. Vanderford, interview.
50. Vanderford, interview.
51. Green, interview.
52. Sandu, interview.
53. "Request for Proposals for the Ohio Manufacturing Talent Expansion for the Defense Industrial Supply Chain for the Manufacturing and Engineering Education Program (MEEP)," Lorain County Community College, December 3, 2020, https://www.lorainccc.edu/about/wp-content/uploads/sites/64/2020/12/MEEP-Research-Data-and-Evaluation-Technical-Assistance_120320-a.pdf.
54. "Training Ohio's Manufacturing Workforce," Ohio TechNet, accessed May 20, 2022, https://ohiotechnet.org/.

CHAPTER 2

1. Kim Parker and Juliana Menasce Horowitz, "Majority of Workers Who Quit a Job in 2021 Cite Low Pay, No Opportunities for Advancement, Feeling Disrespected," Pew Research Center, March 9, 2022, https://www.pewresearch.org/fact-tank/2022/03/09/majority-of-workers-who-quit-a-job-in-2021-cite-low-pay-no-opportunities-for-advancement-feeling-disrespected/; Abha Bhattarai, "Job Openings Hit New Records, While 4.5 Million Americans Quit or Changed Jobs in March, Reflecting Labor Market Strength," *Washington Post*, May 3, 2022, https://www.washingtonpost.com/business/2022/05/03/jobs-quits-hires-march-2022/.

2. "MGCCC History," Mississippi Gulf Coast Community College, accessed March 20, 2022, https://mgccc.edu/about/mgccc-history/.

3. "Campuses," Mississippi Gulf Coast Community College, accessed March 20, 2022, https://mgccc.edu/contact/campuses/.

4. "QuickFacts: Gulfport City and Jackson City, Mississippi," United States Census Bureau, accessed March 20, 2022, https://www.census.gov/quickfacts/fact/table/jacksoncitymississippi,gulfportcitymississippi/PST045221.

5. "Poverty Status in the Past 12 Months," 2020: ACS 5-Year Estimates Subject Tables, United States Census Bureau, accessed March 20March 20, 2022, https://data.census.gov/cedsci/table?t=Poverty&g=0100000US,%240400000.

6. "Completion Rates, 2015–2019 (Completing college, adults 25 and older)," United States Department of Agriculture Economic Research Service, accessed March 20, 2022, https://www.ers.usda.gov/topics/rural-economy-population/employment-education/rural-education/.

7. Michelle Liu, "Wage Gap for Mississippi's Black Women One of Nation's Largest," *Mississippi Today*, August 7, 2018, https://mississippitoday.org/2018/08/07/campaign-seeks-equity-for-mississippis-black-women-who-earn-56-cents-for-each-dollar-white-men-get/.

8. *College Affordability Profile 2020—Mississippi* (Atlanta: Southern Regional Education Board, January 2021). https://www.sreb.org/sites/main/files/file-attachments/2021_state_afford_profile_ms.pdf.

9. "Community Colleges FAQs: How Many Students Are Enrolled in Community Colleges?," Community College Research Center, Teachers College, Columbia University, accessed March 20, 2022, https://ccrc.tc.columbia.edu/community-college-faqs.html#:~:text=In%20fall%202020%2C%20about%204.8,3.1%20million%20were%20part%2Dtime.

10. "QuickFacts: Pascagoula City, Mississippi," United States Census Bureau, accessed March 20, 2022, https://www.census.gov/quickfacts/pascagoulacitymississippi.

11. "Percent Change in Population, 2010–20: Mississippi," United States Department of Agriculture Economic Research Service, accessed March 20, 2022, https://data.ers.usda.gov/reports.aspx?ID=17827.

12. "Mississippi Featured Facts," in *SREB Fact Book on Higher Education* (Atlanta: Southern Regional Education Board, 2021), https://www.sreb.org/sites/main/files/file-attachments/mississippi21.pdf.

13. "Excelerate 2030: The Strategic Plan for Mississippi Gulf Coast Community College," Mississippi Gulf Coast Community College, accessed March 20, 2022, https://mgccc.edu/wp-content/uploads/2020/09/MGCCC-Excelerate-2030.pdf.

14. "Mississippi Occupational Projections for Gulf Coast Community College District," Mississippi Department of Employment Services, accessed March 20, 2022, https://mdes.ms.gov/media/63543/oep_ccd_mgc.pdf.

15. "Who We Are," Ingalls Shipbuilding, accessed March 20, 2022, https://ingalls .huntingtoningalls.com/who-we-are/#:~:text=Ingalls%20Shipbuilding%20is%20 located%20in,of%20both%20Mississippi%20and%20Alabama.

16. "Chevron Pascagoula Refinery: Fact Sheet," Chevron, April 2021, https://pascagoula .chevron.com/-/media/pascagoula/about/documents/CHEVRON_PASCAGOULA _REFINERY_FACT_SHEET_2021.pdf.

17. "Our History," Mississippi Power, accessed March 20, 2022, https://www.mississippi power.com/company/about-us/our-history.html.

18. "About Us," Keesler Air Force Base, accessed March 20, 2022, https://www.keesler .af.mil/Units/81st-Training-Wing/.

19. "About Singing River," Singing River Health System, accessed March 20, 2022, https:// singingriverhealthsystem.com/about-singing-river/#:~:text=Singing%20River%20 Health%20System%20is,in%20more%20ways%20than%20one.

20. Anna Roy, "Coastal Mississippi Sees 2021 Tourism Boom," *Coastal Mississippi*, July 16, 2021, https://www.gulfcoast.org/articles/post/coastal-mississippi-sees-2021-tourism -boom/.

21. "Student Enrollment Trends," Mississippi Gulf Coast Community College, accessed March 20, 2022, https://mgccc.edu/college-factbook-enrollment/.

22. Information provided by Mississippi Gulf Coast Community College in an email on July 26, 2022.

23. "Student Enrollment Trends" accessed March 20, 2022, https://mgccc.edu/college -factbook-enrollment.

24. "Student Enrollment Trends."

25. "Student Enrollment Trends."

26. "Student Enrollment Trends."

27. Information provided by Mississippi Gulf Coast Community College in an email on July 26, 2022.

28. "MGCCC Provides Kits and Laptops for Remote Learning to Career and Technical Education Students," Mississippi Gulf Coast Community College, December 7, 2020, https://mgccc1.rssing.com/chan-52313611/article507-live.html.

29. "Excelerate 2030."

30. Information provided by Mississippi Gulf Coast Community College in an email on July 26, 2022.

31. "Programs: Schools," Mississippi Gulf Coast Community College, accessed March 20, 2022, https://mgccc.edu/programs/schools/.

32. "Career Center," Goodwill of South Mississippi, accessed March 20, 2022, https://www .goodwillsms.org/careercenter.

33. "Simulation and Game Design Technology," Mississippi Gulf Coast Community College, accessed March 20, 2022, https://mgccc.edu/programs/schools/engineering -mathematics-data-science-it/simulation-and-game-design-technology/.

34. "Staying Eligible," Federal Student Aid, accessed March 20, 2022, https://studentaid .gov/understand-aid/eligibility/staying-eligible.

35. "Apprenticeship Grant Awarded to Mississippi," Mississippi Department of Employment Security, July 14, 2020, https://mdes.ms.gov/news/2020/07/14/apprenticeship-grant -awarded-to-mississippi/.

36. "What Will I Receive After I Complete a Registered Apprenticeship Program?," United States Department of Labor, accessed March 20, 2022, https://www.apprenticeship.gov /help/what-will-i-receive-after-i-complete-registered-apprenticeship-program.

37. "Jump Start Your Career Through Apprenticeship," United States Department of Labor, accessed March 20, 2022, https://www.apprenticeship.gov/career-seekers.
38. "Ingalls Apprentice School," Ingalls Shipbuilding, accessed March 20, 2022, https://ingalls.huntingtoningalls.com/careers/apprentice/.
39. "Apprenticeship Programs," Mississippi Gulf Coast Community College," accessed March 20, 2022, https://mgccc.edu/programs/community-education/apprenticeship-programs/.
40. "Ingalls Apprentice School."
41. "Haley Reeves Barbour Maritime Training Academy," Mississippi Gulf Coast Community College, accessed March 20, 2022, https://mgccc.edu/campus/haley-reeves-barbour-maritime-training-academy/.
42. "LPN to RN (Hybrid)," Mississippi Gulf Coast Community College, accessed March 20, 2022, https://mgccc.edu/programs/schools/nursing-health-professions/nursing/lpn-to-rn-transitional/.
43. "QEP Embracing Essential Skills—Student Learning Outcome Submission Form," Mississippi Gulf Coast Community College, accessed March 20, 2022, https://mgccc.edu/quality-enhancement-plan/assessment-2/qep-embracing-essential-skills-student-learning-outcome-submission-form/.
44. Sara DiNatale, "Mississippi Has a Workforce Problem. New State Agency Accelerate Mississippi Aims to Solve It," *Mississippi Today*, July 29, 2021, https://mississippitoday.org/2021/07/29/mississippi-workforce-problem-new-state-agency-accelerate-mississippi-aims-to-solve-it/.
45. "Workforce Development (WIOA) Partners in MS," Governor's Office State Workforce Investment Board (SWIB), February 24, 2020, https://s3.documentcloud.org/documents/7205755/Final-Workforce-Development-Spreadsheet-V2-0.pdf.
46. "Mississippi Employment Report," Joint Economic Committee, January 25, 2022, https://www.jec.senate.gov/cards/__employment-updates/Mississippi%20Employment%20Report.html.
47. Anna Wolfe, "What Is Mississippi Getting for $350 Million a Year in Workforce Development? Leaders Vow to Find Out," *Mississippi Today*, September 23, 2020, https://mississippitoday.org/2020/09/23/what-is-mississippi-getting-for-350-million-a-year-in-workforce-development-leaders-vow-to-find-out/.
48. Wolfe, "What Is Mississippi Getting."
49. DiNatale, "Mississippi Has a Workforce Problem."
50. "About AccelerateMS," Accelerate Mississippi, accessed March 20, 2022, https://acceleratems.org/.
51. Anna Wolfe, "Mississippi Works? Four Years Later, State Has Used Just One-Tenth of $50 Million Workforce Fund," *Mississippi Today*, August 28, 2020, https://mississippitoday.org/2020/08/28/mississippi-works-four-years-later-state-has-used-just-one-tenth-of-50-million-workforce-fund/.
52. Kaitlin Howell and Thao Ta, "Mississippi Governor Provides Update on Workforce Development Efforts," WJTV, April 20, 2022, https://www.wjtv.com/news/politics/focused-on-politics/mississippi-governor-discusses-workforce-development-efforts/.
53. "Perkins V," Perkins Collaborative Resource Network, accessed March 20, 2022, https://cte.ed.gov/legislation/perkins-v.
54. "Student Satisfaction Inventory Results," Mississippi Gulf Coast Community College, accessed March 20, 2022, https://mgccc.edu/office-institutional-research-effectiveness/factbook-and-dashboards/general-college-reports/college-factbook-student-satisfaction-results-online-traditional/.

55. Lindsay Knowles and Chet Landry, "MGCCC Changes Name of Jefferson Davis Campus in Gulfport," WLOX, July 27, 2020, https://www.wlox.com/2020/07/27/mgccc-changes-names-jefferson-davis-campus/.
56. "Some Chosen to Design Mississippi Flag Without Confederate Symbol," KMBC, July 15, 2020, https://www.kmbc.com/article/some-chosen-to-design-mississippi-flag-without-confederate-symbol/33330254.
57. Veronica Stracqualursi, "Mississippi Ratifies and Raises Its New State Flag over the State Capitol for the First Time," CNN, July 13, 2021, https://www.cnn.com/2021/01/12/politics/mississippi-new-state-flag-flown/index.html.

CHAPTER 3

1. Hallie Busta, "Partnership of the Year: A 4-Year Cloud Degree Pathway," Higher Ed Dive, December 9, 2019, https://www.highereddive.com/news/cloud-degree-amazon-george-mason-nova-dive-awards/566275/.
2. Amazon, "Amazon Selects New York City and Northern Virginia for New Headquarters," press release, November 13, 2018, https://press.aboutamazon.com/news-releases/news-release-details/amazon-selects-new-york-city-and-northern-virginia-new.
3. James Finley, "How a Few NoVA Urbanists Made Up This Place Called National Landing—and Landed Amazon HQ2," *Northern Virginia Magazine*, March 8, 2022, https://northernvirginiamag.com/home/real-estate/2022/03/08/national-landing-amazon-hq2/.
4. Kyaw Khine, "A Greater Number of Jobs Require More Education, Leaving Middle-Skill Workers with Fewer Opportunities," StatChat, May 10, 2021, https://statchatva.org/2019/05/10/a-greater-number-of-jobs-require-more-education-leaving-middle-skill-workers-with-fewer-opportunities/.
5. NOVA, *NOVA Strategic Plan 2017–2023: Pathway to the American Dream* (Northern Virginia Community College, February 18, 2018), https://www.nvcc.edu/about/mission/strategic-plan2017-2023.pdf.
6. "Northern Virginia Community College Case Study," AWS, 2018, https://aws.amazon.com/solutions/case-studies/NOVA/.
7. Alexis Gravely, "Washington Watch: Community College Earmarks," *Community College Daily*, March 16, 2022, https://www.ccdaily.com/2022/03/washington-watch-community-college-earmarks/.
8. Rich Miller, "AWS Plans Massive Expansion of Its Northern Virginia Cloud Cluster," Data Center Frontier, August 3, 2020, https://datacenterfrontier.com/aws-plans-massive-expansion-of-its-northern-virginia-cloud-cluster/.
9. Jim Naughton, "NOVA: The Emergence of the Community College," *Washington Post*, November 14, 1999, https://www.washingtonpost.com/wp-srv/local/edureview/higher119901.htm.
10. "Headcount/FTES: NOVA Fact Book," Northern Virginia Community College, accessed May 20, 2022, https://www.nvcc.edu/osi/oir/fact-book/headcount-21.html.
11. "Headcount/FTES." We also referenced internal institutional data for 2021–2022.
12. Dan Burrows, "The 10 'Real' Richest Counties in the U.S.," Kiplinger, August 2, 2021, https://www.kiplinger.com/real-estate/603232/the-real-richest-counties-in-the-us.
13. Northern Virginia Health Foundation, *Getting Ahead: The Uneven Opportunity Landscape in Northern Virginia* (Alexandria: Northern Virgina Health Foundation, November 27, 2017), https://novahealthfdn.org/resources/getting-ahead-the-uneven-opportunity-landscape-in-northern-virginia.

14. NOVA, "NOVA Named as a Top Producer of Fulbright U.S. Scholars," press release, March 1, 2022, https://www.nvcc.edu/news/press-releases/2022/fulbright-scholars.html.

15. NOVA, *Northern Virginia's Information Technology Workforce 2020* (Northern Virginia Community College, Office of Strategic Partnerships and Workforce Innovation, 2020), https://www.nvcc.edu/workforce/docs/IT_WorkforceBrief2020-Final.pdf.

16. Meghan McNally, *Washington: Number One in College Degrees* (Washington, DC: Brookings Institution, June 2003), https://www.brookings.edu/wp-content/uploads /2016/06/01_education_technology_shearer.pdf.

17. *Northern Virginia's Information Technology Workforce 2020.*

18. "Virginia," in *Labour Market Relevance and Outcomes of Higher Education in Four US States: Ohio, Texas, Virginia and Washington* (Paris: OECD, 2020), https://www.oecd -ilibrary.org/sites/85e17923-en/index.html?itemId=%2Fcontent%2Fcomponent%2F8 5e17923-en.

19. "Virginia."

20. "Virginia."

21. NOVA, *NOVA Strategic Plan 2017–2023.*

22. Dr. Anne Kress, interview with author, March 25, 2022.

23. In addition to its internal LMI team, NOVA benefits from Virginia's newly formed Office of Education Economics (OEE). This is a first-in-the-nation effort to create an independent and rigorous data source to support the commonwealth's talent development efforts. Most recently, the Virginia OEE has been tasked with working closely with the Virginia Community College System on an annual review of the Get Skilled, Get a Job, Give Back (G3) program approvals process. This means taking a close look at program eligibility and ensuring that the academic programs Virginia's community college system is offering G3 support to are aligned with high-demand occupations.

24. Brittney Davidson, Tess Henthorne, Karthik Ilakkuvan, Linda Perlstein, Keith Witham, and Joshua Wyner, *The Workforce Playbook: A Community College Guide to Delivering Excellent Career and Technical Education* (Washington, DC: Aspen Institute, 2019), https:// highered.aspeninstitute.org/wp-content/uploads/2019/06/The-Workforce-Playbook _Final.pdf.

25. Busta, "Partnership of the Year."

26. Michelle Van Noy and Katherine Hughes, *A Snapshot of the Shifting Landscape of Non-credit Community College Workforce Education* (Piscataway, NJ: Rutgers Education and Employment Research Center, 2022), https://smlr.rutgers.edu/sites/default/files /Documents/Centers/EERC/Snapshot%20of%20Shifting%20Landscape%20Issue% 20Brief.FINAL_0.pdf.

27. AT&T, "AT&T and NOVA Launch IT Apprenticeship Program," press release, August 17, 2021, https://about.att.com/story/2021/northern_virginia_community_college_it _apprenticeship_program.html.

28. Mary Beth Lakin, Deborah Seymour, Christopher J. Nellum, and Jennifer R. Crandall, *Credit for Prior Learning: Charting Institutional Practice for Sustainability* (Washington, DC: American Council on Education, 2015), https://www.acenet.edu/Documents /Credit-for-Prior-Learning-Charting-Institutional-Practice-for-Sustainability.pdf.

29. "NOVA SySTEMic," NOVA, accessed May 20, 2022, https://www.nvcc.edu/systemic/.

30. NOVA, "Northern Virginia Community College and the United States Marine Corps Partner, in Collaboration with Amazon Web Services, to Develop a New Course of Study," press release, July 10, 2019, https://www.nvcc.edu/news/press-releases/2019 /nova-usmc-aws.html.

31. "NOVA Continues Partnership with AWS with Cloud Ambassadors," NOVA, May 14, 2020, https://www.nvcc.edu/news/featured-articles/2020/aws-cloud-ambassadors.html.

32. NOVA, "Governor Ralph Northam Signs 'G3' Bill at NOVA," press release, March 29, 2021, https://www.nvcc.edu/news/press-releases/2021/Northam-Signs-G3.html.

33. NOVA, "Northern Virginia Community College and the Northern Virginia Chamber of Commerce Launch Workforce Index," press release, October 6, 2021, https://www.nvcc.edu/news/press-releases/2021/Workforce-Index.html.

34. NOVA, *Northern Virginia's Information Technology Workforce 2020.*

35. NOVA, "Northern Virginia Community College Cloud Computing Students Participate on Panel for Amazon Web Services' Public Sector Summit in Washington, D.C.," press release, June 17, 2019, https://www.nvcc.edu/news/press-releases/2019/aws-sector-summit.html.

36. Charles T. Evans, *The Changing Face of Higher Education: Northern Virginia Community College and the Corporatization of Higher Education* (Charles T. Evans, May 2019), https://www.ctevans.net/Papers/CommunityCollegeChanges.pdf.

CHAPTER 4

1. Jamai Blivin and Merrilea Mayo, *Shift Happens @ Pima Community College: The Future of Working and Learning* (Santa Fe, NM: Innovate+Educate, 2019), https://issuu.com/innovate-educate/docs/shift_pima_sept2019.

2. Blivin and Mayo, *Shift Happens.*

3. "Quick Facts," Pima Community College, 2021, https://www.pima.edu/about-pima/quick-facts/index.html.

4. Blivin and Mayo, *Shift Happens.*

5. Blivin and Mayo.

6. "QuickFacts: Pima County, Arizona," US Census Bureau, 2021, https://www.census.gov/quickfacts/fact/table/pimacountyarizona/LND110210.

7. "QuickFacts: Pima County, Arizona."

8. Quarterly Census of Employment and Wages, 2010–2020 Annualized Employees in Private NAICS Industries in Pima County, AZ, Bureau of Labor Statistics. Tables generated via https://data.census.gov; see https://data.bls.gov/PDQWeb/en, accessed May 2022.

9. Quarterly Census.

10. *Economic Development Plan 2019–2021* (Pima County, AZ, 2019), https://webcms.pima.gov/UserFiles/Servers/Server_6/File/Government/Economic%20Development/2019%20Economic%20Development%20Plan.pdf.

11. *Economic Development Plan.*

12. "QuickFacts: United States," US Census Bureau, 2021, https://www.census.gov/quickfacts/US.

13. "QuickFacts: Pima County, Arizona."

14. "QuickFacts: United States."

15. "QuickFacts: United States."

16. *Workforce Development Transformation* (Tucson, AZ: Pima Community College—Planning Governance, and Finance, 2022).

17. Blivin and Mayo, *Shift Happens.*

18. "College Organization," Pima Community College, July 2021, https://www.pima.edu/about-pima/leadership-policies/college-organization/index.html.

19. Blivin and Mayo, *Shift Happens.*

20. Blivin and Mayo.
21. *Enrollment Trend Report* (Tucson, AZ: Pima County Community College, 2021), https://www.pima.edu/about-pima/reports-data/student-reports/docs-enrollment/2010-2021-headcount-and-ftse-trend-report.pdf.
22. "Metrics, Indicators, and Ratios: Financial Indicators," Pima Community College, Office of Finance and Administration, 2021, https://www.pima.edu/administration/finance/docs/pcc-financial-indicators-fy2011-2020.pdf.
23. Blivin and Mayo, *Shift Happens.*
24. "Proposition 481 Impact," Pima Community College, 2021, https://pima.edu/about-pima/leadership-policies/chancellor/annual-report/2021/impact.html.
25. Blivin and Mayo, *Shift Happens.*
26. *Comprehensive Economic Development Strategy* (Tucson, AZ: City of Tucson, 2015), https://www.tucsonaz.gov/files/business/CEDS2015.pdf.
27. *Comprehensive Economic Development Strategy.*
28. *Comprehensive Economic Development Strategy.*
29. Quarterly Census of Employment and Wages, 2010–2020 All Employees in Total Covered Total, All Industries for All Establishment Sizes in Arizona—Statewide, NSA, Bureau of Labor Statistics, series ID ENU0400010010. Tables generated via https://data.census.gov; see https://data.bls.gov/PDQWeb/en>, accessed May 2022.
30. Quarterly Census of Employment and Wages, 2010–2020 Annual Averages, All Establishment Sizes, Total Covered, 10 Total, All Industries, All States and U.S., Bureau of Labor Statistics. See https://www.bls.gov/cew/publications/employment-and-wages-annual-averages/, accessed May 2022.
31. Quarterly Census of Employment and Wages, 2010-2020 All Employees in Total Covered Total, All Industries for All Establishment Sizes in Pima County, Arizona, NSA, Bureau of Labor Statistics, series ID ENU0401910010. Tables generated via https://data.census.gov; see https://data.bls.gov/PDQWeb/en, accessed May 2022.
32. Quarterly Census, series ID ENU0901910010.
33. Quarterly Census, series ID ENU0901910010.
34. *Economic Development Plan.*
35. *Economic Development Plan.*
36. "Job Training and Employment Base Development," in *Pima County Economic Development Plan—Update through 2018* (Pima County, AZ, 2018), https://webcms.pima.gov/UserFiles/Servers/Server_6/File/Government/Economic%20Development/Econ%20Dev%20Plan%20Update%202018/3418%20-%20EDP%202016%20Chapter%2012%20loRes.pdf.
37. "In-Demand Industries and Occupations," Arizona Commerce Authority, March 2022, https://www.azcommerce.com/oeo/labor-market/in-demand-jobs/.
38. "Job Training and Employment."
39. "Job Training and Employment."
40. "All Sectors: County Business Patterns, Including ZIP Code Business Patterns, by Legal Form of Organization and Employment Size Class for the U.S., States, and Selected Geographies: 2020," US Census Bureau, accessed April 28, 2022, https://data.census.gov/cedsci/table?t=Employment%20Size&g=0500000US04019.
41. *Workforce Development Transformation.*
42. "Centers of Excellence," Pima Community College, accessed May 20, 2022. https://pima.edu/about-pima/locations/coe/.
43. "Centers of Excellence."

44. "Governor Ducey Attends Launch of Pima Community College-Caterpillar Education Partnership," Office of the Arizona Governor, accessed November 27, 2022, https://az governor.gov/governor/news/2018/08/governor-ducey-attends-launch-pima-community -college-caterpillar-education.
45. "High School Career Connect," Pima Community College, https://www.pima.edu /admission/dual-enrollment/career-connect.html.
46. James Palacios (director of dual enrollment and high school programs at Pima), email communication, May 11, 2022.
47. Blivin and Mayo, *Shift Happens.*
48. Pima Community College, "PCC to Help at Least 600 Southern Arizonans Find Jobs in Key Economic Sectors," press release, October 26, 2020, https://pima.edu/news/press -releases/2020/202010-26-cc-growth-engine-fund.html.
49. Pima Community College, "PCC to Help."
50. Valerie Taylor, "How Pima Community College Is Using Universal Design + Access to Create Micro-Pathways for the Success of Adult Learners," Education Design Lab, October 14, 2021, https://eddesignlab.org/news-events/how-pima-community-college -is-using-universal-design-access-to-create-micro-pathways-for-the-success-of-adult -learners/.
51. Taylor, "Using Universal Design."
52. Pima Community College, "PCC to Help."
53. "Prior Learning Assessment (PLA)," Pima Community College, https://www.pima.edu /academics-programs/credit-prior-learning/index.
54. "Prior Learning Assessment (PLA)."
55. "Prior Learning Assessment (PLA)."
56. "About Work-Based Learning," JFF, https://www.jff.org/what-we-do/impact-stories /center-for-apprenticeship-and-work-based-learning/about-work-based-learning/.
57. Pima Community College, *Work-Based Learning Guide* (Tucson, AZ: Pima Community College, Employer Engagement and Career Services, n.d.), https://www.pima.edu /business-industry/workforce/docs/210319-employer-guide.pdf.
58. Larry Buchanan, Amanda Cox, Gregor Aisch, and Kevin Quealy, "Some Colleges Have More Students from the Top 1 Percent than the Bottom 60. Find Yours," *New York Times*, January 18, 2017, https://www.nytimes.com/interactive/2017/01/18/upshot /some-colleges-have-more-students-from-the-top-1-percent-than-the-bottom-60.html? action=click&contentCollection=Opinion&module=Trending&version=Full*ion =Marginalia&pgtype=article.
59. Blivin and Mayo, *Shift Happens.*
60. "Prior Learning Assessment (PLA)."
61. Lee Lambert, "In a Post-Covid World, Community Colleges Must Bridge the Gap Between Education and Employment," Pima Community College, 2020, https:// www.pima.edu/about-pima/leadership-policies/chancellor/chancellor-publications /202006-in-a-post-covid-world-community-colleges.html.

CHAPTER 5

1. "District Quick Facts," San Jacinto College, last updated January 2022, https://www .sanjac.edu/sites/default/files/22-339_Mktg_Quick%20Facts%20Certified%20Update %20Dec_D_Fall_hires_0.pdf.
2. "2017 Aspen Institute Rising Star Award," San Jacinto College, 2017, https://www .sanjac.edu/aspen-2017.

3. *Opportunity News*, San Jacinto College, July 4, 2021, https://www.sanjac.edu/sites /default/files/inline-files/Opportunity-News-JULY-2021.pdf.

4. *Comprehensive Annual Financial Report: For the Fiscal Years Ended August 31, 2018 and 2017*, San Jacinto Community College District (Pasadena, TX: Department of Fiscal Affairs, 2018), https://www.sanjac.edu/sites/default/files/SJCD-CAFR-2018 .pdf.

5. "Houston—The Woodlands—Sugar Land," in At the Heart of Texas: Cities' Industry Clusters Drive Growth (Dallas: Federal Reserve Bank of Dallas, December 2018), 34–39, https://www.dallasfed.org:443/research/heart/houston.

6. "Houston: Economy: Major Industries and Commercial Activity: Incentive Programs— New and Existing Companies," City-Data.com, https://www.city-data.com/us-cities /The-South/Houston-Economy.html.

7. "Houston: Economy."

8. "Houston–The Woodlands–Sugar Land."

9. "Chancellor," San Jacinto College, https://www.sanjac.edu/about-san-jac/leadership /chancellor.

10. "Student Success Stats," San Jacinto College, https://www.sanjac.edu/reflections-decade /student-success-stats.

11. "2017 Aspen Institute Rising Star Award"; "Student Success Stats."

12. "Chancellor."

13. "Top 5 Community College in the Nation," San Jacinto College, https://www.sanjac. edu/aspen-2021.

14. Andrea Vasquez, "San Jacinto College Wins National Award for Outstanding STEM Education," San Jacinto College Newsroom, September 30, 2020, https://www.sanjac .edu/news/san-jacinto-college-wins-national-award-outstanding-stem-education.

15. "Current Data and Reports," San Jacinto College, https://www.sanjac.edu/about-san-jac /college-operations/research-and-institutional-effectiveness/current-data-and-reports.

16. "Current Data and Reports."

17. San Jacinto College, "Taking Responsibility for Student Outcomes After Graduation," Aspen Institute, College Excellence Program, May 18, 2021, https://highered.aspen institute.org/idea/taking-responsibility-for-student-outcomes-after-graduation/.

18. San Jacinto College, "Taking Responsibility."

19. "Maritime," San Jacinto College, https://www.sanjac.edu/programs-courses/maritime.

20. "Maritime."

21. "Maritime."

22. "Maritime Testimonials," San Jacinto College, accessed May 20, 2022, https://www .sanjac.edu/programs-courses/maritime.

23. *Center for Petrochemical, Energy, and Technology: Programs and Information* (Houston: San Jacinto College, n.d.), https://www.sanjac.edu/sites/default/files/inline-files/CPET -Programs-Brochure_0.pdf.

24. *Center for Petrochemical, Energy, and Technology.*

25. *Center for Petrochemical, Energy, and Technology.*

26. "Houston Industries," Greater Houston Partnership, https://www.houston.org/why -houston/industries/all-industries.

27. "Aerospace EDGE Center, " San Jacinto College, https://www.sanjac.edu/programs -courses/cpd/your-career/aerospace-program/aerospace-edge-center.

28. "Aerospace EDGE Center."

29. John DeLapp, "San Jac: Program for BS in Nursing Serves Growing Workforce Needs," *Houston Chronicle*, May 3, 2022, https://www.houstonchronicle.com/home/article/San -Jac-Program-for-BA-in-nursing-serves-growing-17144248.php.
30. "Houston–The Woodlands–Sugar Land."
31. DeLapp, "Program for BS in Nursing."
32. "Strategic Leadership," San Jacinto College, https://www.sanjac.edu/about-san-jac /leadership/strategic-leadership.
33. "Strategic Leadership."
34. Davis Jenkins and Lauren Pellegrino, *Collaborating to Break Down Barriers to Student Success: Guided Pathways Reforms at San Jacinto College* (New York: CCRC of Teachers College, Columbia University), 20.
35. Jenkins and Pellegrino, *Collaborating to Break Down Barriers*, 20.
36. Jenkins and Pellegrino, 20.
37. "Top 5 Community College in the Nation."
38. Jenkins and Pellegrino, *Collaborating to Break Down Barriers*.
39. Jenkins and Pellegrino.
40. Jenkins and Pellegrino.
41. Jenkins and Pellegrino.
42. "Credit for Prior Learning (CPL)," San Jacinto College, https://publications.sanjac.edu /general-information/student-information/student-grades-records/credit-examination/.
43. Jenkins and Pellegrino, *Collaborating to Break Down Barriers*, 20.
44. Jenkins and Pellegrino, 20.
45. Jenkins and Pellegrino, 20.
46. "Houston Guided Pathways to Success," University of Houston, https://www.uh.edu /provost/university/houstongps/index.
47. Jenkins and Pellegrino, *Collaborating to Break Down Barriers*, 20.
48. Amanda Fenwick, "Aspen Institute Names San Jac a Top 10 Finalist," San Jacinto College, September 13, 2016, https://www.sanjac.edu/aspen-prize.
49. Jenkins and Pellegrino, *Collaborating to Break Down Barriers*, 20.
50. Colleen Ferguson, "San Jacinto College Named Finalist with Distinction for National Aspen Prize for Community College Excellence," *Community Impact*, May 29, 2021, https://communityimpact.com/houston/bay-area/education/2021/05/29/san-jacinto -college-named-finalist-with-distinction-for-national-aspen-prize-for-community -college-excellence.
51. Fenwick, "Aspen Institute Names San Jac a Top 10 Finalist."
52. Colleen Ferguson, "San Jacinto College to Expand Scholarship Offerings for Class of 2022 Using MacKenzie Scott Donation," *Community Impact*, November 12, 2021, https://communityimpact.com/houston/bay-area/education/2021/11/12/san-jacinto -college-to-expand-scholarship-offerings-for-class-of-2022-using-mackenzie-scott -donation/.
53. Yvette Orozco, "San Jac Marks 60th Year with New Programs," *Houston Chronicle*, December 28, 2021, https://www.houstonchronicle.com/neighborhood/pasadena/article /San-Jac-marks-60th-year-with-new-programs-16734324.php.
54. Brenda Hellyer, "Strategic Plan: Chancellor's Message," San Jacinto College, https:// www.sanjac.edu/about-san-jac/overview/strategic-plan.
55. "Diversity, Equity, and Inclusivity," San Jacinto College, https://www.sanjac.edu/CDI.
56. "San Jac Innovations," San Jacinto College, https://www.sanjac.edu/san-jac-innovations.

57. "San Jac Innovations."
58. Tiffany Pennamon, "San Jacinto College Students Get Free Online Textbooks and 'Aid Like a Paycheck,'" *Diverse: Issues in Higher Education*, June 28, 2018, https://www.diverseeducation.com/latest-news/article/15102769/san-jacinto-college-students-get-free-online-textbooks-and-aid-like-a-paycheck.
59. "Diversity, Equity, and Inclusivity."
60. Amanda Fenwick, "San Jacinto College Chancellor Honored with Prestigious Quasar Award," San Jacinto College, January 31, 2020, https://www.sanjac.edu/news/san-jacinto-college-chancellor-honored-prestigious-quasar-award.

CHAPTER 6

1. Amy Liu, "Remaking Economic Development: The Markets and Civics of Continuous Growth and Prosperity," Brookings, February 29, 2016, https://www.brookings.edu/research/remaking-economic-development-the-markets-and-civics-of-continuous-growth-and-prosperity/.
2. Stephanie Marken, "Half in U.S. Now Consider College Education Very Important," Gallup, December 30, 2019, https://www.gallup.com/education/272228/half-consider-college-education-important.aspx.
3. "Public Viewpoint: COVID-19 Work and Education Survey," Strada Education Network, June 10, 2020, https://stradaeducation.org/report/pv-release-june-10-2020/.
4. Anthony P. Carnevale, Ban Cheah, Neil Ridley, and Jeff Strohl, *Good Jobs that Pay Without a BA* (Washington, DC: Georgetown University Center on Education and the Workforce, 2017), https://repository.library.georgetown.edu/bitstream/handle/10822/1047863/CEW_Good-jobs-that-pay-without-a-BA.pdf?sequence=1&isAllowed=y.
5. "Fast Facts 2022," American Association of Community Colleges, 2022, https://www.aacc.nche.edu/research-trends/fast-facts/.
6. Shalin Jyotishi, "Community Colleges Foster Racial and Gender Equity in the Manufacturing Workforce," *New America*, June 29, 2022, http://newamerica.org/education-policy/edcentral/community-colleges-foster-racial-and-gender-equity-in-manufacturing-workforce/.
7. "College Enrollment Declines Appear to Be Worsening," *Clearinghouse Today Blog*, National Student Clearinghouse, May 26, 2022, https://www.studentclearinghouse.org/nscblog/undergraduate-enrollment-falls-662000-students-in-spring-2022-and-1-4-million-during-the-pandemic/.
8. "College Enrollment Declines."
9. *State Higher Education Finance: FY 2021* (Boulder, CO: State Higher Education Executive Officers Association, 2022), https://shef.sheeo.org/wp-content/uploads/2022/06/SHEEO_SHEF_FY21_Report.pdf; Victoria Yuen, *The $78 Billion Community College Funding Shortfall* (Washington, DC: Center for American Progress, October 2020), https://www.americanprogress.org/wp-content/uploads/2020/10/Community-College-Shortfall6.pdf.
10. Alex Coccia, "Successful Community College Acceleration Program Should Be Expanded Through the FY22/23 Budget," *Be the Voice* (blog), Children's Defense Fund Ohio, April 2, 2021, https://cdfohio.org/cdf_oh_blog/successful-community-college-acceleration-program-should-be-expanded-through-the-fy22-23-budget/.
11. Betty Marquez Rosales, "California Colleges Now Have Centers to Help Students with Basic Needs like Food and Housing," EdSource, August 11, 2022, https://edsource.org

/2022/california-colleges-now-have-centers-to-help-students-with-basic-needs-like-food
-and-housing/676568?amp=1.

12. Mitchell Lingo, Robert Kelchen, Dominique Baker, Kelly Rosinger, Justin Ortagus, and
Jiayao Wu, "The Landscape of State Funding Formulas for Public Colleges and Universities," InformEd States, December 2021, https://informedstates.org/policy-briefs-feed/the
-landscape-of-state-funding-formulas-for-public-colleges-and-universities-jtbcg-z3g7x.

13. "Fast Facts 2022."

14. Mark M. D'Amico, Grant B. Morgan, Zoë Mercedes Thornton, and Vladimir Basis,
"Noncredit Education Enrollment and Outcomes: Exploring the 'Black Box' of Noncredit Community College Education," *Career and Technical Education Research* 45, no.
2 (2020): 17–37.

15. Peter Riley Bahr, Yiran Chen, and Rooney Columbus, "Community College Skills
Builders: Prevalence, Characteristics, Behaviors, and Outcomes of Successful Non-
Completing Students Across Four States," *Journal of Higher Education*, June 28, 2022,
1–36, https://doi.org/10.1080/00221546.2022.2082782.

16. R. M. Romano and M. M. D'Amico, "How Federal Data Shortchange the Community
College," *Change: The Magazine of Higher Learning* 53, no. 4 (2021): 22–28.

17. For an example, see the Voluntary Framework of Accountability, a national effort
designed by the American Association of Community Colleges (AACC) to serve as an
accountability framework for community colleges with success measures tailored for this
sector of higher education. You can view the measures at https://vfa.aacc.nche.edu/.

18. Kevin Dougherty and Marianne Bakia, *The New Economic Development Role of the Community College* (New York: CCRE of Teachers College, Columbia University, 1999).

ACKNOWLEDGMENTS

The coeditors would like to thank the following individuals, without whose participation this project would not have been possible:

Our five case authors—Rachel Boroditsky, Sakshee Chalwa, Hayley Glatter, Furman Haynes, and Analisa Sorrells—for fitting this project into their busy student lives and embracing the assignment with such energy and commitment.

Our extraordinary HPoW staff colleagues—Isaiah Baldiserra, Ali Epstein, and Melanie Shimano—for providing critical support at every step of the project. We are lucky to work with such talented colleagues and can't wait to see the stamp these future leaders will leave on the field.

Our faculty colleagues—Peter Blair, David Deming, and Joe Fuller—for their thought partnership and participation in our June 2022 convening of colleges and states.

Tamar Jacoby, president of Opportunity America, who served as project advisor and whose 2020 report, *The Indispensable Institution: Reimagining Community College*, served as a springboard for this project.

Jayne Fargnoli, editor in chief at Harvard Education Press, who has been an essential partner in bringing this book into the world.

This work would not have been possible without the dedicated support from a private foundation. We would also like to acknowledge the Capital One Foundation, a generous supporter of the Project on Workforce's research agenda on the connection between education and the labor market.

The case authors would like to thank the following college partners for their time and efforts supporting the project research. These individuals participated in interviews or provided other critical support to the development of our cases:

Lorain County Community College: Marcia Ballinger, Cindy Kushner, Kelly Zelesnik, Terri Sandu, Tracy Green, Marisa Vernon White, Thomas Benjamin, Johnny Vanderford, Tony Gallo, Michael Fitzpatrick, and Ethan Karp.

Mississippi Gulf Coast Community College: Mary Graham, Jonathan Woodward, Jordan Sanderson, Erin Riggins, John Poelma, Adam Swanson, Suzana Brown, Gayle Brown, Tonya Neely, Ryan Miller, Jessica Lewis, Michael Leleux, Tommy Murphy, Ann Holland, Ruth Montana, Damita Caldwell, Tripp Harrison, Carlin Taylor, and Deeneaus Polk.

Northern Virginia Community College: Anne Kress, Steve Partridge, Chad Knights, and Dana Fallon.

Pima Community College: Aaron Ball, Amanda Abens, Calline Sanchez, Crispin Jeffrey-Franco, David Dore, Denise Kingman, Greg Wilson, Ian Roark, Joe Snell, Laurie Kierstead-Joseph, Lee Lambert, Nancy Johnson, Nicola Richmond, and Robert Walker.

San Jacinto College: Brenda Hellyer, Laurel Williamson, and Allatia Harris.

ABOUT THE EDITORS
AND CONTRIBUTORS

Robert B. Schwartz (coeditor), emeritus professor of practice at the Harvard Graduate School of Education, has played a variety of roles in education: high school teacher and principal; education advisor to the mayor of Boston and the governor of Massachusetts; education director of the Pew Charitable Trusts; and founding president of Achieve, Inc.

In 2011, he coauthored an influential report calling for more attention to career and technical education: *Pathways to Prosperity: Meeting the Challenge of Preparing Young Americans for the 21st Century*. In 2012, with Nancy Hoffman from Jobs for the Future, he cofounded a national network of states and regions to act upon the analysis and recommendations outlined in the Pathways report. In October 2017, Hoffman and Schwartz published *Learning for Careers* (Harvard Education Press), their participant/observer implementation report on the first five years of the Pathways to Prosperity Network. Schwartz is currently senior advisor to Harvard's interfaculty Project on Workforce and senior research fellow at Harvard Kennedy School.

Rachel Lipson (coeditor) cofounded the Project on Workforce at Harvard alongside Bob Schwartz, Harvard Business School Professor Joseph Fuller, and Harvard Kennedy School Professor David Deming. As the project's inaugural director, Lipson spearheads the project's cross-disciplinary and cross-sector research agenda and strategy, including partnerships with state and federal agencies. Before this role, Lipson served as director of special projects at Year Up, a US workforce development training provider that creates pipelines for diverse talent into high-demand jobs at top companies. Previously, while enrolled as a joint MBA/MPP candidate and Rubenstein Fellow

189

at Harvard, Lipson studied the connection between California's community college system and economic mobility. Her research was awarded the Kennedy School's Frederick Fischer Prize for outstanding research on social policy. She is also a past recipient of the Harvard Certificate of Distinction and Excellence in Teaching for the Economics Department's political economy of globalization course.

Prior to Harvard, Lipson focused on human capital and economic development topics, including roles at the World Bank, JPMorgan Chase, and the Obama presidential campaign. She frequently serves as an advisor and commentator on labor market and education issues, including on the Biden-Harris Economic Policy Committee. Her writing has been published in the *Boston Globe, Washington Post*'s *Wonkblog, Newsweek, The Hill, Forbes, Huffington Post*, and RealClearPolicy, and her work has been featured by C-SPAN, Bloomberg, *The Economist*, CNBC, New America, NPR, and *MIT Technology Review.*

Hayley Glatter is a master of public policy candidate at the Harvard Kennedy School and a research assistant at the Project on Workforce at Harvard. Previously, Hayley was a communications associate at the Community College Research Center (CCRC), which is based at Teachers College, Columbia University. She was also an education journalist at *The Atlantic* and covered politics and breaking news at *Boston Magazine*. Hayley holds a bachelor's degree in journalism and history, as well as a certificate in integrated marketing from Northwestern University.

Analisa Sorrells is a master of public policy candidate at the Harvard Kennedy School and a research assistant at the Project on Workforce at Harvard. Previously, Analisa was the chief of staff and associate director of policy with EducationNC, a nonprofit media organization covering K–12 education and community colleges in North Carolina. Analisa holds a bachelor's degree in public policy with a minor in media and journalism from the University of North Carolina at Chapel Hill.

Furman Haynes is currently a master of business administration candidate and Goldsmith Fellow at Harvard Business School. He is also a research assistant at the Project on Workforce. Previously, Furman cofounded CityWorks

DC, a nonprofit that helps connect young people of color to good jobs in the Washington, DC, region. In his role as cofounder and chief of staff, Furman worked with business leaders and city government officials to implement programs and shift policies. He graduated summa cum laude from Princeton University with a degree in politics.

Rachel Boroditsky is a master of business administration candidate at Harvard Business School and a research assistant at the Project on Workforce at Harvard. Previously, Rachel was an engagement manager at McKinsey & Company, where she worked with higher education institutions and systems on strategic and operational topics. She was also an associate at Imagine Worldwide, a nonprofit that delivers tablet-based literacy and numeracy programs in Africa and Asia. Rachel holds a degree in economics and mathematical methods in the social sciences from Northwestern University.

Sakshee Chawla is a master of public policy graduate of the Harvard Kennedy School of Government and a research assistant at the Project on Workforce at Harvard. Previously, Sakshee worked at an education research and technology firm, where she studied topics including student success, retention, and equity. She developed a toolkit for universities to promote student and faculty mental health, and she analyzed learning loss expected from school closures during the pandemic. During her time at Harvard Kennedy School, Sakshee has served as a technical writer and researcher at the Institutional Antiracism and Accountability (IARA) Project and on the teaching team for economics and statistics courses. Sakshee holds a bachelor of arts in economics and psychology from Smith College.

INDEX

Abens, Amanda, 117
academic planning software, 139
Accelerate MS, 54–55
Adult Basic Education for College and Career
    (ABECC) programs, 113–114
ADVANCE, 79
Advanced CNA program, 80, 91
advising, 42
advisory committees
    Chancellor's Advisory Council, 120, 126
    community engagement and, 53
    data analytics used by, 146
    development of, 126–127
    employers serving on, 17, 25, 112
aerospace program, 129–130, 136
affordability, 97, 142–143. *See also* earn-
    and-learn model
Aid Like a Paycheck program, 145
Alternus, Steve, 125
alumni, 142, 147–148
Amazon, 69–70, 72, 78–79, 91
American Council on Education, 82
applied learning. *See* apprenticeship pro-
    grams; earn-and-learn model;
    work-based learning experiences
Applied Technology Academy, 110
apprenticeship programs
    benefits of, 49
    for incumbents, 50
    at LCCC, 17
    at MGCCC, 30–31, 47–53
    at NOVA, 82
articulation agreements, 141–142
Aspen Institute, 78

bachelor of science in nursing (BSN)
    program, 130
bachelor's degrees, public view of, 151
Ballinger, Marcia, 15, 152
Beard, Peter, 136, 147
Berman, Mike, 79, 87
board memberships, 16, 90, 111, 120, 131,
    152–153
brain drain, 35
Brown, Gayle, 47–48, 53
Brown, Suzana, 38–39
BSN (bachelor of science in nursing)
    program, 130
Building IT Futures program, 20

career advancement. *See* workforce
    development
Career by Design initiative, 18–21
Career Readiness and Leadership Institute, 86
career readiness centers, 42–43
career services
    Career by Design initiative, 18–21
    flipped model for, 69, 83, 120, 139
    integration of, 157–158
    restructuring of, 85
    whole college approach to, 6, 14, 18–19,
        69, 84, 157–158
career technical education (CTE). *See also*
    credit versus noncredit
    advisory committees for, 53
    credit versus noncredit distinction and,
        38–42
    health metrics for CTE program assess-
        ment, 31, 56–64